The Veil

The
Veil

by

Brian C. Hales

ISBN: 1-55517- 487-6
v.1

Published by Bonnevile Books

Distributed by:
925 North Main, Springville, UT 84663 • 801/489-4084

CFI | Publishing and
Distribution Since 1986

Cedar Fort, Incorporated
CFI Distribution • CFI Books • Council Press • Bonneville Books

Typeset by Virginia Reeder
Cover design by Adam Ford
Cover design © 2000 by Lyle Mortimer

Printed in the United States of America

Table of Contents

Chapter One

The Veil and Eternity

While serving as a missionary, years ago, I would often ask investigators three important questions: "Where did I come from?" "Why am I here?" "Where am I going after this life?" The questions seemed pertinent enough, but most of the individuals I spoke with seemed to have little concern regarding their answers. Eternity seemed to be mostly a non-issue.

I frequently wondered why such basic questions are so easily ignored. Part of the reason might come from the many demands on our time which we experience. Our jobs and family responsibilities, the phone, newspaper, Church duties and spiritual concerns all seem to tug at us. Thank heavens for daily planners right?

Regardless, our lives often seem so frantically invested in the present minute. How readily our thoughts and concerns seem to shrink into the moment. How seldom they may stretch back to decades before or forward to the millennia to come. It is easy to live day-to-day mostly unaware of eternity.

There are many reasons we are so effortlessly distracted from eternal realities. Preeminent among them is the veil. The veil hides eternity and eternal things, thus permitting us to flounder in the mortal sea of cares and concerns. Yet it need not be so. By examining the veil and how it affects us, we can transcend the lives we currently lead and become as Abraham. While traveling to Canaan, he wrote: "Eternity was our covering and our rock and our salvation, as we journeyed" (Abr. 2:16).

ETERNITY

Discussions about the veil and eternity are rarely found within orthodox Christian denominations. Very good reasons exist to explain why this is so. For them, everything found on the other side of the veil is incomprehensible. They believe that eternity exists as a *timeless*, *space-less* and *matter-less* state. For mortals on earth, it is simply beyond our ability to apprehend. According to their teachings, God dwells within this eternity and is equally unfathomable.

The *incomprehensible* nature of the orthodox Christian "eternity" and God provides little motivation for mainstream Christians to examine things beyond the veil in any detail (philosophers excluded). Equally unappealing is any study of the veil itself which separates us from this incomprehensible realm.

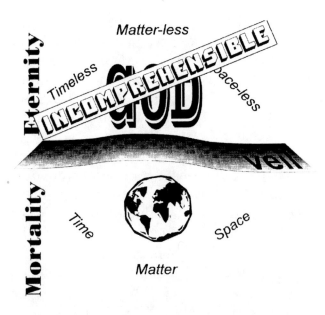

Eternity as Described by Orthodox Christianity

The Restored Gospel and "Eternity"

Latter-day Saints enjoy a great advantage over other Christ-centered religions. Through the restoration, we have come to know that eternity is quite different from the unintelligible entity described by orthodox Christian theology.

"Eternity" in LDS theology is a word generally used to describe all that exists outside of mortality. The veil is the dividing line. However, the veil does not separate a "timeless" eternity from a time-infested realm. Instead, the veil demarcates the threshold between segments of eternity. Our God exists within eternity, but He is surrounded by time (D&C 130: 4, 7). *Time-lessness* is unrelated to eternity as taught in the doctrines of the restored Church. It is unreal, the figment of human imagination.

Eternity is also filled with "matter" which occupies "space." Some of the matter is *spirit* matter which is hidden from our senses by the veil. Nonetheless, spiritual matter is just as real as the physical matter we touch and see. Joseph Smith taught: "All spirit is matter, but it is more fine or pure, and can only be discerned by purer eyes" (D&C 131:7), eyes which can peer through the veil.

While many aspects of eternity remain confusing to mortals on earth, numerous details are within our comprehension. Thanks to the restored Gospel, many aspects of the premortal eternity and the postmortal eternity are available to us even now. Hence it is a great deal more fun and useful to scrutinize than is the eternity (and the veil) as described by orthodox Christianity.

PIERCING THE VEIL

Since the veil separates us from God and eternity, we might conclude that it is our enemy. In fact, the veil is our friend. Undoubtedly we agreed to abide by its limitations in some premortal setting perhaps because we somehow understood the great opportunities it would create for us on earth.

The veil is necessary if mortality is to serve as a probationary state for earth's inhabitants. Elder Neal A. Maxwell observed: "Without the veil, for instance, we would lose that precious insulation which keeps us from a profound and disabling homesickness that would interfere with our mortal probation and maturation. Without the veil, our brief, mortal walk in a darkening world would lose its meaning..." (*All These Things Shall Give Thee Experience*, p. 10).

Piercing the Veil—Learning of God

The veil is naturally very thick for most of us. However, it is not completely impenetrable. It appears certain that our Heavenly Father wants us to pierce it. For millennia, He has been communicating through it by giving us "revelations." And what is being revealed when revelations come? Often it is eternity. Commonly, prophetic utterances simply reveal things found outside the veil or they convince us of the need to prepare for things outside the veil. In either case, the veil is thinned with God's help to illuminate eternal realities.

Perhaps the greatest reality we may snatch from eternity is a knowledge of God. We know He is very different from the incomprehensible essence of orthodox Christianity. It is His intent that we learn of Him: "I give unto you these sayings that you may understand and know how to worship, and *know what you worship*" (D&C 93:19; italics added). He wants us to even know Him: "And this is life eternal, *that they might know thee* the only true God, and Jesus Christ, whom thou hast sent" (John 17:3; italics added).

It is not presumptuous to search the scriptures and the writings of modern prophets to learn about God, His dwelling place and all eternity. The scriptures even promise that the veil separating us from God may someday be lifted, allowing us to plainly see Him: "Therefore, sanctify yourselves that your minds become single to God, and the days will come that you shall see him; for he will unveil his face unto you..." (D&C 88:68).

Learning about eternity brings other blessings. It can expand our views until we perceive the world with an *eternal perspective.* The value of an eternal perspective comes as it reduces our trials and challenges in their intensity and their ability to dominate us. An eternal perspective strengthens our resolve to perform righteously as we come to cherish eternal promises. An eternal perspective spawns patience, meekness and all other Christ-like attributes.

Piercing the Veil—Learning of Eternity

Learning of eternity helps us prepare for all that is to come. In each of our lives, the moment will arrive when the veil will dissolve and we will find ourselves surrounded by portions of eternity which now escape us. Whether it is sooner or later, it is inevitable. What better way to prepare for that great moment than to study the eternal truths about eternity which have been revealed to us by God's prophets?

We are eternal beings; therefore, learning about eternity comes naturally. "When true doctrines are advanced, though they may be new to the hearers, yet the principles contained therein are perfectly natural and easy to be understood, so much so that the hearers often imagine that they had always known them," instructed Brigham Young (*Discourses of Brigham Young*, p. 160). President Joseph F. Smith taught: "All those salient truths which come home so forcibly to the head and heart seem but the awakening of the memories of the spirit. Can we know anything here that we did not know before we came?" (*Gospel Doctrine*, p. 13).

Nonetheless, the veil remains. It constantly separates us from the knowledge of eternal things. Such knowledge can rescue us from so many of the troubles we experience here on earth.

Eternity is Now

This discussion has firmly placed "eternity" outside of the veil. However, such a characterization is technically inaccurate because we are even now in eternity. "The time we now occupy is in eternity; it is a portion of eternity. Our present life is just as much a life in eternity as the life of any being can possibly be" declared Brigham Young (JD 9:168). He also explained: "We were in the [premortal] spirit world, and we came here into this time, which is in eternity; we are just as much in eternity now, as we shall be millions of years hence. But it is time measured to finite beings, and it is changeable, and we call it temporal" (*Discourses of Brigham Young*, p. 461). So at this very moment, eternity surrounds us and engulfs us. That makes "now" a part of eternity. Therefore, to truly understand "now," we must understand eternity. The veil is the key.

2

Understanding the Veil

One universal consequence of mortality is the veil. It enshrouds our minds from the very first second we are born upon this earth. It is incredibly constant and its effect upon our lives is immensely profound. It appears that the veil is designed with love by our Heavenly Father in order to create a very special environment where we can grow and progress. Apparently the veil successfully veils its own reality besides hiding eternity from our consciousness. Consequently, the veil might currently affect us in ways we have yet to realize.

Examining the veil of eternity suggests that it has different segments, each obscuring from our awareness a distinct spiritual realm which lies hidden from us in eternity. Paul observed: "[F]or the things which are seen are temporal; but the things which are not seen are eternal" (2 Cor. 4:18).

THE VEIL AND THE PREMORTAL EXISTENCE

The first aspect of the veil we will consider is the portion concealing the premortal world. At birth, the veil settles over our minds, suppressing our memories of the ages and eons we lived in the premortal realms with our Heavenly Father. There we experienced growth and learning and participated in the Grand Council. Yet the veil has caused us to forget everything.

Remembering Our Heavenly Family

One recollection we would gladly recall involves our eternal relationship with our Heavenly Parents. Brigham Young taught: "I want to tell you, each and every one of you, that you are well acquainted with God our Heavenly Father, or the great Elohim. You are all well acquainted with Him, for there is not a soul of you but what has lived in His house and dwelt with Him year after year" (*Discourses of Brigham Young*, p. 50).

Elder Harold B. Lee taught:

> Now, the fact that you and I are here in mortal bodies is evidence that we were among those who were in that great concourse of organized intelligence; we knew God, our Father. He was our Heavenly Father; we were sired by Him. We had a Heavenly Mother... Born of a Heavenly Mother, sired by a Heavenly Father, we knew Him, we were in His house, and we knew His illustrious Son, who was to come here and redeem mankind as a part of the plan of salvation. What did He mean, then, when He said, "And this is life eternal that they might know thee the only

true God, and Jesus Christ, whom thou hast sent"? (John 17:3) It is to regain that knowledge, then, and to go back where we once were that becomes the great quest of all of us (*The Teachings of Harold B. Lee*, p. 22).

During premortality, our relationship with Heavenly Father and Heavenly Mother was undoubtedly the most important personal association we enjoyed.

It appears that in the heavenly realms, we were surrounded by billions of our spirit siblings. It seems certain that we learned to love others, developing friendships which were deep and satisfying. Eliza R. Snow penned the following words as a part of the hymn, "O My Father": "For a wise and glorious purpose, Thou hast placed me here on earth. And withheld the recollection, Of my *former friends* and birth" (*Hymns*, #292; italics added). President Joseph F. Smith explained how death in mortality allows us to return to enjoy those associations. In a funeral address he noted: "The spirit of our beloved sister in taking its departure from this world, is born again into the spirit world, returning there from the mission it has been performing in this state of probation, having been absent a few years from father, mother, kindred, friends, neighbors, and from all that was dear; it has returned nearer to the homecircle, to old associations and scenes, much in the same way as a man who comes home from a foreign mission, to join again his family and friends and enjoy the pleasures and comforts of home" (*Gospel Doctrine*, p. 440; see also *The Teachings of Harold B. Lee*, p. 52).

Premortal Growth and Learning

From the moment of our spiritual creation, Father granted each of us our free agency. In the premortal world we exercised it to progress. Elder Bruce R. McConkie explained: "We all lived as spirit beings, as children of the Eternal Father, for an infinitely long period of time in the premortal existence. There we developed talents, gifts, and aptitudes; there our capacities and abilities took form..." (*A New Witness for the Articles of Faith*, p. 34). He also wrote: "Being subject to law, and having their agency, all the spirits of men, while yet in the Eternal Presence, developed aptitudes, talents, capacities, and abilities of every sort, kind, and degree. During the long expanse of life which then was, an infinite variety of talents and abilities came into being. As the ages rolled, no two spirits remained alike" (*The Mortal Messiah*, 1:23).

The most important choices we made in the preexistence involved our spirituality. "The greatest and most important talent or capacity that any of the spirit children of the Father could gain is the talent of spirituality," taught Bruce R. McConkie (*A New Witness for the Articles of Faith*, p. 512). Elder Howard W. Hunter explained: "Our spirits were begotten by God and have had an extensive period of growth and development in the spirit world, where we came to know God and to comprehend the nature of spiritual realities" (*The Teachings of Howard W. Hunter*, p. 12).

The development of spirituality apparently occurred in conjunction with a premortal "Church organization." Elder Joseph Fielding Smith observed: "During the ages in which we dwelt in the premortal state, we not only developed our various characteristics and showed our worthiness and ability, or the lack of it, but we were also where such progress could be observed. It is reasonable to believe that there was a Church organization there. The heavenly beings were living in a perfectly arranged society. Every person knew his place. Priesthood, without any question, had been conferred and the leaders were chosen to officiate. Ordinances pertaining to that preexistence were required and the love of God prevailed" (*The Way to Perfection*, pp. 50-51).

Perhaps the premortal Church organization was called "The Church of Jesus Christ of *Premortal* Saints," or the "Church of Jehovah," or the "Church of the Firstborn." Within that organization we participated in priesthood ordinances and ordinations to sacred offices. Joseph Smith explained: "Every man who has a calling to minister to the inhabitants of the world was ordained to that very purpose in the Grand Council of heaven before this world was" (*Teachings of the Prophet Joseph Smith*, p. 365). Ezra Taft Benson instructed: "The calling and testing of men for assignment of responsibility in the great work of salvation is, no doubt, going on on both sides of the veil. The calling of men to sacred office is not confined to earth life only. There is organization, direction, and assignment in pre-earth life and in post-earth life also" (*Teachings of Ezra Taft Benson*, p. 21).

The Grand Council and Beyond

After allowing an almost infinite period to grow and progress, our Heavenly Father held a Grand Council. Our individual premortal labors created differences and disparity between us. "[W]e were not equal in the Grand Council; we were not equal after the Grand Council" declared President J. Reuben Clark (CR, October 1956, pp. 83-84). Regardless, we all attended a Grand Council Meeting. There we heard the Father's plan for our salvation presented and watched as Jesus Christ, the Firstborn Spirit, offered Himself as the Redeemer. "At the first organization in heaven we were all present, and saw the Savior chosen and appointed and the plan of salvation made, and we sanctioned it," Joseph Smith taught. (See *Words of Joseph Smith*, p. 60.) At the sight we "sang together" and "shouted for joy" (Job 38:7). We also saw Satan rebel and witnessed his expulsion from heaven. Possibly we were participants in the heavenly throng who "wept over" his loss (D&C 76:26).

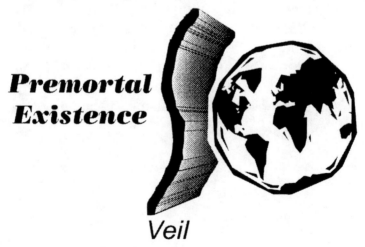

Premortal Existence

Veil

Life in the premortal realm after the Grand Council must have been different from life before. Satan and his opposing forces had been dispatched to earth. The remaining spirits were all aware that they were destined to endure mortality on this planet. Whether the earth was immediately formed and spirits sent here we are not told. Possibly we were required to wait still another eon or two. Eventually however, the time came for our spirit brothers and sisters to leave that place and experience their mortal birth. Adam and Eve left first. Then the time came for each of us personally to depart. Our spirits burst through the veil into mortality but we were forced to leave our recollections of our former lives behind.

THE VEIL CONCEALING GOD AND HIS ANGELS

The veil over our minds does more than just conceal our premortal memories. A portion of it also hides God from our senses. We saw Him face-to-face in the premortal heavens but He is now concealed from us. Nevertheless He is not far away. "But behold, verily, verily, I say unto you that mine eyes are upon you. I am in your midst and ye cannot see me" (D&C 38:7). "Lift up your hearts and be glad, for I am in your midst, and am your advocate with the Father..." (D&C 29:5; see also 6:32 etc.). Brigham Young explained: "I wish the people could realize that they walk, live, and abide in the presence of the Almighty. The faithful shall have eyes to see as they are seen, and you shall behold that you are in the midst of eternity and in the presence of holy beings, and be enabled ere long to enjoy their society and presence. You are greatly blessed" (*Discourses of*

Brigham Young, pp. 454-455). Were the veil to be rent today, we would see how literally "in our midst" the Lord really is.

The scriptures assure us that God's angels are also with us during our mortal probation. When a Syrian king went to war against Israel, he sought to capture the prophet Elisha to prevent Elisha and his prophetic gifts from assisting Israel. The king brought his army and surrounded Elisha and Elisha's servant:

> Therefore sent he thither horses, and chariots, and a great host: and they came by night, and compassed the city about.
>
> And when the servant of the man of God was risen early, and gone forth, behold, an host compassed the city both with horses and chariots. And his servant said unto him, Alas, my master! how shall we do?
>
> And he answered, Fear not: for they that be with us are more than they that be with them.
>
> And Elisha prayed, and said, Lord, I pray thee, open his eyes, that he may see. *And the Lord opened the eyes of the young man; and he saw: and, behold, the mountain was full of horses and chariots of fire round about Elisha* (2 Kings 6:14-17; italics added).

God
(& His Angels)

Veil

The Lord has promised: "And whoso receiveth you, there I will be also, for I will go before your face. I will be on your right hand and on your left, and my Spirit shall be in your hearts, and mine angels round about you, to bear you up" (D&C 84:88). President Joseph F. Smith concluded: "I believe we move and have our being in the presence of heavenly messengers and of heavenly beings. We are not separated from them" (*Gospel Doctrine*, p. 430). Brigham Young observed: "There is much in my presence besides those who sit here, if we had eyes to see the heavenly beings that are in our presence" (*Discourses of Brigham Young*, p. 42). Joseph Smith taught: "The spirits of the just are exalted to a greater and more glorious work; hence they are blessed in their departure to the world of spirits. Enveloped in flaming fire, they are not far from us, and know and understand our thoughts, feelings, and motions, and are often pained therewith" (*Teachings of the Prophet Joseph Smith*, p. 326).

A segment of the veil conceals deity and all things divine. Piercing this veil to recapture the knowledge of God's reality constitutes the ultimate focus of all our faith.

THE VEIL HIDING SATAN AND HIS FOLLOWERS

Another portion of the veil hides other spirit entities such as the devil and his followers. The Lord has warned us concerning them: "Behold, verily I say unto you, that there are many spirits which are false spirits, which have gone forth in the earth, deceiving the world" (D&C 50:2). They comprise an entire third of the spirits originally destined to be born upon this earth.

The War In Heaven

John the Revelator viewed the war in heaven and gave us this description:

> And there appeared another wonder in heaven; and behold a great red dragon...
> And his tail drew the third part of the stars of heaven, and did cast them to the earth...
> And there was war in heaven: Michael and his angels fought against the dragon; and the dragon fought and his angels,

And prevailed not; neither was their place found any more in heaven.

And the great dragon was cast out, that old serpent, called the Devil, and Satan, which deceiveth the whole world: *he was cast out into the earth, and his angels were cast out with him...*

Therefore rejoice, ye heavens, and ye that dwell in them. *Woe to the inhibitors of the earth and of the sea! for the devil is come down unto you, having great wrath,* because he knoweth that he hath but a short time (Rev. 12:3-4, 7-9, 12; italics added).

"There is a war between Satan and God," explained President George Q. Cannon, a member of the First Presidency in 1894:

We are brethren and sisters of Satan as well as of Jesus. It may be startling doctrine to many to say this; but Satan is our brother. Jesus is our brother. We are the children of God. God begot us in the spirit in the eternal worlds. This fight that I speak of arose, as we are told, over the question as to how man should work out his earthly probation in a tabernacle of flesh and bones and obtain redemption. Satan differed from God, and he rebelled. We are told in the scriptures that he drew after him one third of the family of God. They thought his plan better than that of the Savior Jesus Christ. From that time until the present he has been struggling to destroy the plans of Jehovah, and to seduce the children of men—his brothers and sisters—from their allegiance to God. Invisible to mortal eyes, he has exerted tremendous power; and because he has been invisible, men have almost denied his existence. Yet the evidence of his existence and of his power is to be seen on every hand. He is determined, if he can, to destroy the plans of God while we are here in a state of probation

(*Collected Discourses* 4:24).

The War Continues on Earth

"[T]he spirit that Lucifer exhibited in heaven has been manifested on the earth," also taught President George Q. Cannon. "When he has had power to influence men and women he has filled them with precisely the same spirit that he manifested in heaven before man came upon the earth" (*Collected Discourses,* 4:301-302). "Be sober, be vigilant; because your adversary the devil, as a roaring lion, walketh about, seeking whom he may devour," warned Peter (1 Peter 5:8).

Satan's rebellion was no surprise to our Heavenly Father. It is an important element in the Plan of Salvation. Brigham Young taught: "Do not imagine that I am in the least finding fault with the Devil. I would not bring a railing accusation against him, for he is fulfilling his office and calling manfully; he is more faithful in his calling than are many of the people" (*Discourses of Brigham Young,* p. 70).

Currently Satan and his followers "encompasseth [us] round about" (D&C 76:29), but we cannot see them because of the veil. They are granted special powers here on earth to "tempt us" (D&C 29:39) but their influence applies only to our physical bodies. Brigham Young explained: "[T]he body is of the earth, and is subject to the power of the Devil, and is under the mighty influence of that fallen nature that is of the earth" (*Discourses of Brigham Young,* p. 70).

All mortals have felt Satan's enticements even though the veil obscures the actual source of all temptation. This is unfortunate because if this veil were somehow removed so that we could understand the ultimate intent of those who induce us to sin, then we might more easily reject their snares just as a thirsty man might decline a glass of clear water if he knew it was skimmed from the top of a sewage drain. President George Q. Cannon observed: "If we could see with our spiritual senses as we now see with our natural senses, we should be greatly shocked at the sight of the influences that prompt us to disobey the counsels of God or the Spirit of the Lord in our hearts. But we cannot see them..." (*Gospel Truth*, p. 65).

A View of the Devil's Angels

On occasion, the veil separating us from Satan will be rent allowing mortals to view or speak with him or some of the third of the hosts of heaven which were cast down with him. One such incident occurred to Elders Isaac Russell, Heber C. Kimball, Willard Richards and Orson Hyde in 1837. Elder Kimball recalled:

[A] vision was opened to our minds, and we could plainly see the evil spirits who foamed and gnashed their teeth at us. We gazed upon them about an hour and a half (by Willard's watch). We were not looking towards the window, but towards the wall. Space appeared before us, and we saw the devils coming in legions, with their leaders, who came within a few feet of us. They came towards us like armies rushing to battle. They appeared to be men of full stature, possessing every form and feature of men in the flesh, who were angry and desperate; and I shall never forget the vindictive malignity depicted on their countenances as they looked me in the eye; and any attempt to paint the scene which then presented itself, or portray their malice and enmity, would be vain (*Life of Heber C. Kimball* by Orson F. Whitney, pp. 130-131).

Elder Hyde provided this description:

[T]heir awful rush upon me with knives, threats, imprecations and hellish grins, amply convinced me that they were no friends of mine... I stood between [Brother Kimball] and the devils and fought them and contended with them face to face, until they began to diminish in number and to retreat from the room. The last imp that left turned round to me as he was going out and said, as if to apologize, and appease my determined opposition to them, "I never said anything against you." I replied to him thus: "It matters not to me whether you have or have not; you are a liar from the beginning! In the name of Jesus Christ depart!" He immediately left, and the room was clear. That closed the scene of devils for that time (ibid. p. 131).

Veil

SATAN
(& His Followers)

THE VEIL AND THE SPIRIT WORLD

Death signals our entrance (or birth) into the Spirit World. With our last heart beat, the veil separating us from the Spirit World dissolves before us to allow passage. "When you lay down this tabernacle, where are you going? Into the spiritual world," taught Brigham Young. Then he asked: "Where is the spirit world? It is right here" (*Discourses of Brigham Young*, p. 376). Who will greet the righteous when they enter that portion of eternity? Again President Young explained: "We have more friends behind the veil than on this side, and they will hail us more joyfully than you were ever welcomed by your parents and friends in this world; and you will rejoice more when you meet them than you ever rejoiced to see a friend in this life..." (*Discourses of Brigham Young*, pp. 379-380). Regarding those who have passed on before us, Elder Wilford Woodruff instructed: "The eyes of all the heavenly hosts are over this people. They are watching us with the deepest anxiety. They understand things better than we do, for our veil is our bodies, and when our spirits leave them we will not have a great way to get into the spirit world" (JD 21:194).

President Joseph Fielding Smith wrote: "The earthly sphere and the sphere of departed spirits are distinct from each other, and a veil is wisely drawn between them. As the living are not, in their normal condition, able to see and converse with the dead so, it is rational to believe, the inhabitants of the spiritual domain are, in their normal condition, shut out from intercourse with men in the flesh. By permission of the Lord, persons on either side of the veil may be manifest to those on the other, but this will certainly be by law and according to the order which God has established" (*Answers to Gospel Questions* 4:110).

Descriptions of the Spirit World

President Jedediah Grant was a member of the First Presidency when he died in 1856. Immediately prior to his death, he shared with Heber C. Kimball, also a member of the First Presidency at that time, his experiences visiting the spirit world.

> He said to me, brother Heber, I have been into the spirit world two nights in succession, and, of all the dreads that ever came across me, the worst was to have to again return to my body, though I had to do it. But O, says he, the order and government that were there! When in the spirit world, I saw the order of righteous men and women; beheld them organized in their several grades, and there appeared to be no obstruction to my vision; I could see every man and woman in their grade and order. I looked to see whether there was any disorder there, but there was none; neither could I see any death nor any darkness, disorder or confusion. He said that the people he there saw were organized in family capacities; and when he looked at them he saw grade after grade, and all were organized and in perfect harmony....
>
> He also spoke of the buildings he saw there, remarking that the Lord gave Solomon wisdom and poured gold and silver into his hands that he might display his skill and ability, and said that the temple erected by Solomon was much inferior to the most ordinary buildings he saw in the spirit world.

In regard to gardens, says brother Grant, "I have seen good gardens on this earth, but I never saw any to compare with those that were there. I saw flowers of numerous kinds, and some with from fifty to a hundred different colored flowers growing upon one stalk." We have many kinds of flowers on the earth, and I suppose those very articles came from heaven, or they would not be here.

After mentioning the things that he had seen, he spoke of how much he disliked to return and resume his body, after having seen the beauty and glory of the spirit world, where the righteous spirits are gathered together (JD 4:135-136).

Concerning the nature of the spirit world, Apostle Parley P. Pratt expressed:

When this spirit departs, the outward tabernacle is said to be dead, that is, the individual who quickened and imparted voluntary motion to the said tabernacle is no longer there. This individual, on departing from its earthly house, repasses the dark vale of forgetfulness, and awakes in the spirit world.

The spirit world is not the heaven where Jesus Christ, His Father, and other beings dwell, who have, by resurrection or translation, ascended to eternal mansions, and been crowned and seated on thrones of power; but it is an intermediate state, a probation, a place of preparation, improvement, instruction, or education, where spirits are chastened and improved, and where, if found worthy, they may be taught a knowledge of the Gospel. In short, it is a place where the Gospel is preached, and where faith, repentance, hope and charity may be exercised; a place of waiting for the resurrection or redemption of the body; while, to those who deserve it, it is a place of punishment, a purgatory or hell, where spirits are buffeted till the day of redemption.

As to its location, it is here on the very planet where we were born; or, in other words, the earth and other planets of a like sphere, have their inward or spiritual spheres, as well as their outward, or temporal. The one is peopled by temporal tabernacles, and the other by spirits. A vail is drawn between the one sphere and the other, whereby all the objects in the spiritual sphere are rendered invisible to those in the temporal (*Key to the Science of Theology*, Chapt. 14, pp. 129-130).

The veil separating us from the spirit world is a portion of the veil we will all become intimately acquainted with, if only for a few seconds. We will all pass through it as we leave mortality to continue our labors in that eternal realm.

Spirit World *(and beyond)*

Veil

THE PLAN OF SALVATION
AND THE VEIL

As we have seen, the different portions of the veil serve to conceal various parts of eternity from our views. If we combine these veils to form a model for mortality, we will discover how fully the earth is encased or enshrouded with a curtain. The veil hides the knowledge of God and the devil, and of the premortal and postmortal worlds from our minds. Together these components comprise the Plan of Salvation.

While living within the veil, it is easy to believe that the Plan of Salvation is truly a "plan," like a set of blueprints which might be tacked onto a wall or spread out across the tail-gate of a contractor's truck. However, as we gain an understanding of things on both sides of the veil, we learn the Plan of Salvation is far more than a map directing us to exaltation. Instead, it constitutes a description of the eternal reality surrounding us. We are immersed within it. The Plan of Salvation is the course of progression in which we are all enrolled whether we want to be or not. It requires each of us to take a short "dip" into the veil to experience earthly "time" and mortality.

God
(& His Angels)

Veil

Premortal
Existence

Spirit
World
(and beyond)

SATAN
(& His Followers)

3

Thinning the Veil

We have learned that the Lord placed the veil over our minds for an important purpose. Accordingly, we cannot individually, or as a group, remove it. No human activity is capable of penetrating it single handedly. No armed force, no congress or president, no nuclear armament, no hurricane, earthquake, lightening or fire can achieve it. However, our Heavenly Father has provided us with a very direct way to dissolve it gradually by degrees. The process is called *faith.*

The apostle Paul described faith using these words: "Now faith is the substance of things hoped for, the evidence of things not seen" (Heb. 11:1). In the Book of Mormon, the Prophet Alma defined it similarly: "And now as I said concerning faith—faith is not to have a perfect knowledge of things; therefore if ye have faith ye hope for things which are not seen, which are true" (Alma 32:21). Alma augments Paul's definition by adding one important concept. The object of our faith must be true. If we combine

Paul's and Alma's definitions, we might conclude that faith is "hoping for things not seen which are true."

For some people, this definition may be less than clarifying because of the word "hope." It might seem as nebulous to our understanding as the word "faith" which we are trying to explain. In place of "hope" we might substitute a form of the word "believe" which we can more easily define. Therefore, a working definition of faith might be: "A belief in things not seen which are true."

We may ask, "What is a belief?" To help us discover the answer, we could compile two lists of ideas or teachings. The first list would contain things we *do* believe. Upon the second we could record a few things we *do not*. By comparing the two lists and identifying the differences in our personal relationship to the things written upon each one, we might recognize what it means to "believe in" something.

Comparing the lists shows that *believing* is not simply studying or talking about something or *claiming* to believe. It goes beyond an intellectual understanding or defense of an idea. To believe something demands that we mentally accept it to be binding upon us. As we embrace it within our minds and hearts, it will be manifested in our lives, in the things we think, say and do.

We might then inquire: "Why are the true things we believe not 'seen'?" The answer is the veil. The *veil* is our source of blindness. It constantly prevents us from easily perceiving eternal truth and bringing it into our private worlds. However, as we exercise faith, the Holy Spirit effectively "thins" the veil but not so we can "see" through it. The spiritual witness we receive convinces us of the truthfulness of true things that our five physical senses still cannot discern.

The process of increasing our faith and believing new eternal truths has several steps.

STEP ONE: AN INTRODUCTION TO TRUTH

The first step requires us to be introduced to true teachings. There may be special occasions where belief can occur "without being brought to know the word" (Alma 32:16). But for most of us, a tangible introduction to the truth will be the first step in generating new levels of faith.

This process was introduced with Adam as he taught truth to his children. Joseph Smith explained: "Adam, thus being made acquainted with God, communicated the knowledge which he had unto his posterity; and it was through this means that the thought was first suggested to their minds that there was a God, which laid the foundation for the exercise of their faith, through which they could obtain a knowledge of his character and also of his glory" (*Lectures on Faith*, 2:31).

Our introduction to truth may occur through many mediums, a book, a speaker, a television program. Usually the most effective is one-on-one teaching which includes bearing testimony regarding the things being taught (see D&C 50:13-22). Regardless, truth must be presented to our eyes and/or ears in a way that at least some part of it can be understood. Then the process has begun.

Sharing "Truth" With Others

Sharing the truths we receive from the heavens with others has been commanded in every dispensation. Adam was commanded to teach his children (Moses 6:55-57). Enoch was sent out as a missionary (Moses 6:32-33, 37, 7:12). Noah preached the gospel (Moses 8:19). And so it is from the beginning—mortal messengers are sent to take gospel truth into all the world. God could assign angels to do it and at times He has, as with Joseph Smith. However, if mortal missionaries are available, the order of heaven seems to demand that they be sent. Examples are plentiful. Paul was directed by the Spirit to teach a man in Macedonia because he prayed (Acts 16). God could have dispatched an angel instead. Cornelius indeed saw an angel, but Peter seems to have been his primary tutor of truth (Acts 10).

Paul spoke of the importance of hearing the truth in order to begin believing it: "For whosoever shall call upon the name of the Lord shall be saved. How then shall they call on him in whom they have not believed? and how shall they believe in him of whom they have not heard? and how shall they hear without a preacher?... So then faith cometh by hearing, and hearing by the word of God" (Romans 10:13-14, 17).

It seems that most of us will need some physical presentation of the truth before we can begin to believe it and increase our faith.

Finding Truth In An Ocean of Information

We currently live in an ocean of information. We are surrounded by facts and communications. It is a very unique environment unlike anything past generations ever experienced. The vast majority of people to have been born on this earth have not even learned how to read and write. Had we lived in the time of Joseph Smith, our access to ideas beyond those contained within the Bible would have been limited. Books were available, but generally scarce. Even finding scratch paper to write the translation of the Book of Mormon upon was a challenge. It was not uncommon for individuals to stay up all night reading in order to finish a particular book because it needed to be returned to its owner the next morning.

With the twenty-first century upon us, we find television, newspapers, magazines, computers and the Internet inundating us with a steady stream of knowledge and ideas. Yet the information is not all of equal worth. Some people may wonder if any of the ideas, among this plethora of information available to us, is true. Possibly they speculate that most of the ideas are equally true or equally false or at least equally useful. Obviously this is not so.

What we discover is that faith can be exercised in any teaching, but faith will increase only if it is focused upon truth. The process of increasing faith helps reveal what is true and what is not.

STEP TWO: MENTAL WORK

The second step to increase faith requires a concerted effort on our part. Joseph Smith explained that faith requires our "mental exertion." "Let us here offer some explanation in relation to faith, that our meaning may be clearly comprehended. We ask, then, what are we to understand by a man's working by faith? We answer—*we understand that when a man works by faith, he works by mental exertion instead of physical* force" (*Lectures on Faith*, 7:3; italics added).

We accomplish this work in two distinct ways.

A Sincere Desire

The first focus of our mental exertion is to generate a desire to know if a specific teaching is true. As we sort through the smorgasbord of ideas placed constantly before our minds, we must pick out a single teaching or several related ideas for special consideration. Simply noticing them or giving them a cursory review will generally not suffice. We must generate a genuine desire to know concerning their truthfulness.

How do we know if our desires are genuine? The key is found in our *willingness to allow our lives to be changed* in accordance with the teaching, should we discover it to be true. Without this level of desire, our efforts to increase our faith will usually be in vain.

It is not uncommon to encounter people who express interest in Christ. However, further conversation may reveal that they are just as fascinated with Him as they are the Bermuda Triangle, UFOs, Big Foot or Taoism, etc. From the start, they may exhibit a great deal of curiosity, but little willingness to actually change their lives. If during their investigations they encounter a special feeling convincing them that some teaching might be true, they often ignore it. Why? Because to acknowledge it would require them to change and they just plain do not want to. These individuals seek for a god who is impersonal and generally stays out of the way. Unremarkably, that is what they find.

Alma in the Book of Mormon encouraged us: "But behold, if ye will awake and arouse your faculties, even to an experiment upon my words, and exercise a particle of faith, yea, even if ye can no more than desire to believe, let this desire work in you, even until ye believe in a manner that ye can give place for a portion of my words" (Alma 32:27). Our *desire* to know prompts us to entertain the possibility that a teaching might be true. Then we must manifest our desire to God in a specific manner. By so doing we position ourselves so we can receive a witness from the other side of the veil. Our efforts must be of sufficient intensity to warrant a divine answer. We can't expect a million-dollar response to a two-cent endeavor.

"Feeling After" the Lord

The second aspect of our mental work requires us to earnestly seek the Lord's spiritual influence. The Apostle Paul understood the basic process through which we develop faith. He told the Athenians that to approach God, we must "*feel after him*, and find him, though he be not far from every one of us" (Acts 17:27; italics added. See also D&C 101:8).

"Feeling after" the Lord necessitates that we earnestly

seek His Spirit as we allow the teachings to permeate our thoughts and feelings. Several specific activities can help us accomplish this. Elder Howard W. Hunter explained: "We must take time to prepare our minds for spiritual things... There must be desire, effort, and personal preparation. This requires, of course, as you already know, fasting, prayer, searching the scriptures, experience, meditation, and a hungering and thirsting after the righteous life" (*The Teachings of Howard W. Hunter*, p. 36).

Prayer

Our desires to thin the veil are manifest as we pray. The prayers we offer may need to rise to a whole new level from those we are used to praying. How can we improve our prayers? Several different aspects may require attention, our preparation, intensity, duration and frequency may all need to be expanded.

Do we prepare for our prayers? If so, what do we do? Preparation may involve cleansing our minds of worldly thoughts and finding a quiet place away from the mainstream of surrounding activities. We might need to avoid praying immediately before retiring to bed or shortly after arising in the morning because of the potential interference from weariness.

Our preparations may include a study of some of the great prayers found in the scriptures. Seeking to understand how our prophets have prayed gives us a pattern for our own prayers. (See 3 Ne. 13:9-13, 19:19-23, 1 Ne. 1:14, Ether 3:2-3.) Proper anticipation of our sacred communications with Deity demonstrates devotion and respect. They can greatly contribute to our overall efforts to pierce the veil.

How intensely do we pray? The emotional investment of our prayers may at times require pleading, yearning, hungering, groping and aching to know. We seek not just to pray, but to pray *mightily* (2 Ne. 4:24). We may do as Alma did as he sought divine assistance. He "labored much in the spirit, wrestling with God in mighty prayer" (Alma 8:10). We might each ask ourselves: "Have I ever 'wrestled with' the Lord?"

When we are not kneeling in prayer or offering up a silent petition, we might remember the counsel: "Yea, and when you do not cry unto the Lord, let your hearts be full, drawn out in prayer unto him continually for your welfare, and also for the welfare of those who are around you" (Alma 34:27), "appeal unto my Spirit. Yea, cleave unto me with all your heart," (D&C 11:18-19); "remain steadfast in your minds in solemnity and the spirit of prayer" (D&C 84:61).

Pondering

Pondering and prayer are closely related. There seems to be a continuum between the two as we follow the admonition to be "drawn out" in prayer even when not praying. The time spent pondering will often require the same preparations as our prayers, but it can also expand to fill moments previously occupied with eternally unimportant thoughts. Dedicating our spare "thinking time" to spiritual things brings great blessings. The Lord encouraged: "Look unto me in every thought" (D&C 6:36), "let all thy thoughts be directed unto the Lord; yea, let the affections of thy heart be placed upon the Lord forever" (Alma 37:36; see also 1 Timothy 4:15).

The temple is an excellent place to ponder. It is the House of the Lord and His Spirit dwells there in abundance. Listening to His Spirit is the focus of our ponderings, our reachings and our search for truths found outside the veil.

Scripture Study

Scripture study is usually an integral element in our quest for increased faith. The scriptures are written in such a way that many different levels of understanding can be found. *There is always more.* Through the Holy Spirit we can recognize answers to questions and identify insights previously overlooked. Usually they will not come to the casual reader. We must avoid simply "reading" the scriptures, but instead follow the Lord's admonition to "search" them (John 5:39).

Worshiping and Service

The Lord has commanded us to attend our Church meetings (D&C 59:9). However, more may be expected than simply parking our bodies inside a church building for a few hours each week. Greater blessings are available if we go to *worship* Jesus Christ through partaking of the Sacrament and renewing our covenants with Heavenly Father. Being open to the Holy Spirit and serving in our callings with all our might is also important.

Our worship must extend throughout the week. We cannot compartmentalize a portion of our time or thoughts to God. They must be constantly foremost in our minds. We must pursue "unseen truth" as a person dying of thirst in the desert searches for water or as a drowning man seeks air. Less intensity in reaching for divine truth usually represents a compromise with the Lord because some portion of our intensity is already expended upon some worldly endeavor.

STEP THREE: RECEIVING THE WITNESS

The third step involves the active participation of the Lord through the Holy Spirit. It occurs as the Lord recognizes our desires and efforts to believe. He has promised: "Ask, and it shall be given you; seek, and ye shall find; knock, and it shall be opened unto you" (Matt. 7:7). More recently He has pledged: "Draw near unto me and I will draw near unto you; seek me diligently and ye shall find me; ask, and ye shall receive; knock, and it shall be opened unto you" (D&C 88:63).

As we introduce a truth into our minds and work to personally learn whether or not it might be true, something happens beyond the veil where all truth originates. The Lord "feels after" us in response to our efforts to "feel after" Him (D&C 112:13). Figuratively, the Holy Spirit facilitates a form of "sympathetic vibration" which occurs between the truth within our minds and the truth outside the veil. The "sympathetic vibrations" cause the truth to expand within us. Apostle John Taylor explained it this way: "When truth shall touch the cords of your heart they will vibrate; then intelligence shall illuminate your mind, and shed [its] lustre in your soul, and you shall begin to understand the things you once knew, but which had gone from you" (*The Mormon*, 29 Aug. 1857; quoted in *The Life and Teachings of Jesus and His Apostles*, p. 331).

Alma compared it to the growth of a seed within our
hearts:

> Now, we will compare the word unto a seed. Now, if
> ye give place, that a seed may be planted in your heart,
> behold, if it be a true seed, or a good seed, if ye do not cast
> it out by your unbelief, that ye will resist the Spirit of the
> Lord, behold, it will begin to swell within your breasts;
> and when you feel these swelling motions, ye will begin to
> say within yourselves—It must needs be that this is a good
> seed, or that the word is good, for it beginneth to enlarge
> my soul; yea, it beginneth to enlighten my understanding,
> yea, it beginneth to be delicious to me.
>
> But behold, as the seed swelleth, and sprouteth, and
> beginneth to grow, then you must needs say that the seed
> is good; for behold it swelleth, and sprouteth, and begin-
> neth to grow. And now, behold, will not this strengthen
> your faith? Yea, it will strengthen your faith: for ye will
> say I know that this is a good seed; for behold it sprouteth
> and beginneth to grow (Alma 32:28, 30).

"Truth carries its own influence and recommends
itself," taught Joseph Smith (*Words of Joseph Smith*, p.
237). Brigham Young observed: "You may know whether
you are led right or wrong, as well as you know the way
home; *for every principle God has revealed carries its own
convictions of its truth to the human mind*, and there is no
calling of God to man on earth but what brings with it the
evidence of its authenticity" (*Discourses of Brigham
Young*, p. 65; italics added). This is the same principle the
Savior referred to when He taught: "If any man will do his
will, he shall know of the doctrine, whether it be of God, or
whether I speak of myself" (John 7:17). If the teaching is
true and we earnestly seek to know it, the Lord will send a
witness regarding it into our hearts.

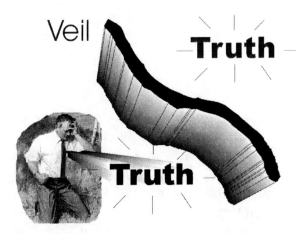

On the other hand, if an idea is false, it will not flourish within us. As Alma taught: "Therefore, if a seed groweth it is good, but if it groweth not, behold it is not good, therefore it is cast away" (Alma 32:32).

"All True Religion Is A Feeling"

How do we know our faith-seed is growing or that our truth is "vibrating" in frequency with eternal truth originating beyond the veil? The answer: "We will *feel* it." We may wonder why we will feel it instead of detecting it with our eyes, ears or other senses.

The answer was demonstrated to me several years ago while reading a book about astronomy. The book contained an article telling of a 1987 occurrence which greatly excited astronomers around the globe. In February of that year, a "supernova" became visible in a large galaxy close to the Milky Way. A supernova is a star which has exploded, causing it's brilliance to increase more than a million times.

It was the first supernova to be visible to the naked eye in almost 400 years and immediately commanded the attention of stargazers around the world. Astronomers and physicists dropped their previous research to study and assess the information provided by the erupted star. As I read about the discovery, I too became excited, feeling some of the enthusiasm the scientists may have experienced in 1987 when they first learned of it.

Suddenly my excitement waned. The text revealed that the supernova was 170,000 *light-years* away from the earth. That meant that the entire scientific community were buzzing over something that happened over 170,000 years ago because it took that long for the light from the explosion to reach earth. This knowledge made the whole episode less intriguing to me. I thought to myself, "This is really *old* news." I realized that 170,000 years ago the star had exploded but we mortals were entirely incapable of discovering the explosion any sooner because the fastest thing our physical senses can detect is light which travels relatively slowly when compared to the distances involved. Admittedly, I am no scientist because I could see little reason to get all animated over something that occurred so long ago.

Even now as we view the night sky, we are deceived by our eyes because what we see is hardly what is actually present in the universe at that moment. Light travels too slowly to truly reveal what is going on out there and our physical bodies are incapable of detecting anything that travels faster than light. If a man wishes to see what the Milky Way actually looked like on the day of his birth, he would need to view it when he turns 75 years old because it takes 75 years for the light to travel from it to us here on earth. Even the light of the sun takes over seven minutes to traverse the millions of miles to warm this planet.

As I learned about this supernova, it was emphasized to me that the senses found in our physical bodies are grossly inadequate to truthfully assess things in the universe and also things of God. Luckily, our Heavenly Father has an infinitely more impressive mode of communication than that discernible by our mortal tabernacles. It intimately involves our feelings.

Some of the plainest verses discussing the way the Lord reveals truth to us while we sojourn on earth were given through Joseph Smith. The Lord instructs us to study, then "you must ask me if it be right, and if it is right I will cause that your bosom shall burn within you; therefore, you shall feel that it is right. But if it be not right you shall have no such feelings" (D&C 9:8-9; italics added). Here we are told we will have a "burning" within the "bosom." Such imagery may be a bit confusing because both terms, "burning" and "bosom," are symbols which may signify different things to different people. However, the Lord also adds quite plainly that we "shall feel that it is right." This may be the key to the matter.

Elder Bruce R. McConkie taught: "All true religion is a feeling" (quoted by Joseph Fielding McConkie, "Understanding Personal Revelation"). We may wonder how this is so. Joseph Smith taught that when the Lord reveals something to us, He does so directly to our spirits: "All things whatsoever God in his infinite wisdom has seen fit and proper to reveal to us, while we are dwelling in mortality, in regard to our mortal bodies, are revealed to us in the abstract, and independent of affinity of this mortal tabernacle, but *are revealed to our spirits precisely as though we had no bodies at all"* (*Teachings of the Prophet Joseph Smith,* p. 533). The Holy Spirit influences our own spirits as they are housed within our physical bodies "as though we had no bodies at all." Yet we do have bodies so it is important for us to understand what sensations we will feel when the Holy Ghost is speaking directly to our spirits within us.

On one occasion, the Lord used the word "signalize" to describe this process. To Joseph Smith, He said that specific revelation would: "be signalized unto you by the peace and power of my Spirit, that shall flow unto you" (D&C 111:8). Elder Boyd K. Packer explained it this way: "Revelation is the process of communication to the spiritual eyes and to the spiritual ears that were ours before our mortal birth" (*The Things of the Soul,* p. 55). The sensations we notice when receiving divine communication are "feelings." Through the Holy Spirit we can "feel" God's influence and even His words (1 Nephi 17:45).

Which Feelings?

Since we have so many feelings, we may wonder where the inspired feelings will be felt within us as truth is manifest to us by the Holy Spirit. The Lord instructed Oliver Cowdery: "Yea, behold, I will tell you in your *mind* and in your *heart,* by the Holy Ghost, which shall come upon you and which shall dwell in your heart. Now, behold, this is the spirit of revelation" (D&C 8:2-3; italics added). We are told that the feelings will occur *within* us, symbolically within our "hearts" and "minds." When they come, the feelings will produce distinct sensations within our bodies and specific thoughts within our brains.

This explanation may still seem inadequate to some. Paul warned: "But the natural man receiveth not the things of the Spirit of God: for they are foolishness unto him: neither can he know them, because they are spiritually discerned" (1 Cor. 2:14). Notwithstanding, it may be impossible to describe the process in greater detail. The Lord may be in the position of an individual who is trying to describe music to a deaf person or the flavor of salt to someone who has never tasted it. The feelings may have to be felt to be truly understood. However, there are some basic observations which may be helpful.

Peace, Joy and Enlightenment

In 1847 Brigham Young had a vision in which the Prophet Joseph Smith appeared to him. Joseph discussed the Spirit of the Lord and the sensations it would cause us to "feel":

Tell the people to be humble and faithful, and be sure to keep the Spirit of the Lord and it will lead them right. Be careful and not turn away the small still voice; it will teach them what to do and where to go; it will yield the fruits of the kingdom. Tell the brethren to keep their hearts open to conviction, so that when the Holy Ghost comes to them, their hearts will be ready to receive it. They can tell the Spirit of the Lord from all other spirits; *it will whisper peace and joy to their souls; it will take malice, hatred, strife and all evil from their hearts; and their whole desire will be to do good, bring forth right-eousness and build up the kingdom of God.* Tell the brethren if they will follow the Spirit of the Lord, they will go right. Be sure to tell the people to keep the Spirit of the Lord (*Journal History*, 23 February 1847; italics added).

Joseph also described the feelings as "pure intelligence," which "may give you sudden strokes of ideas" (*Teachings of the Prophet Joseph Smith,* p. 151). To Hyrum Smith the Lord said: "Verily, verily, I say unto you, I will impart unto you of my Spirit, which shall enlighten your mind, which shall fill your soul with joy" (D&C 11:13). Words like "enlighten," "joy" and "peace" are commonly used to describe the *feelings* which convey revelation from God. Paul taught: "the fruit of the Spirit is love, joy, peace, long suffering, gentleness, goodness, faith, meekness, temperance..." (Galatians 5:22-23). The witness we receive as we strive to increase our faith will usually come as these very feelings (see also D&C 6:15, 23).

Joseph Smith explained that the process of embracing truth as being more than something that "feels" good. He said it also "tastes" good: "This is good doctrine. It tastes good. I can taste the principles of eternal life, and so can you. They are given to me by the revelations of Jesus Christ; and I know that when I tell you these words of eternal life as they are given to me, you taste them, and I know that you believe them. You say honey is sweet, and so do I. I can also taste the spirit of eternal life. I know it is good; and when I tell you of these things which were given me by inspiration of the Holy Spirit, you are bound to receive them as sweet, and rejoice more and more" (*Teachings of the Prophet Joseph Smith,* p. 355). "When I have a problem," Joseph also explained, "I pray about it and then in due time, ideas come into my mind, such a logical flow of ideas attended by such a burning in my bosom, that I know they are of God and I dictate them to my secretary..." (Quoted by Truman Madsen, "Timeless Questions, Gospel Insights" lecture 6).

Some people may be unconvinced and unimpressed with these observations. They might believe that God's communications to His children must be grander and more impressive to the five physical senses. Feelings may seem too routine, too day-to-day, too mundane to possibly be divinely inspired. Unfortunately individuals who believe this way may go through life without the benefit that inspired "feelings" could give them.

False "Feelings"

Learning which "feelings" are from the Lord usually takes time and experience. Like any other talent, spirituality and receiving revelation require effort and even training. There are forces which can deceive us. Our own passions, moods and emotions can lead us astray. When we experience extremes of moods such as frustration, anger, happiness or suffering, our "feelings" may be difficult to sort out. Detecting the Lord's influence can also require special attention. Elder Neal A. Maxwell has written: "Great care must be exercised so that, as leaders and members, we do not pass off our personal preferences as the Lord's principles; we must not confuse our religious hobbies with His orthodoxy! There is a difference between a spiritual impression and a personal obsession. The latter may merely mask a long-held drive to be heard or to be vindicated..." (*Notwithstanding My Weakness*, p. 110).

Besides our own emotions, Satan is here on earth with his followers. As we have learned, they have been granted the power to "tempt" us. His enticements generate "feelings" within our physical bodies. Brigham Young taught: [T]he devil... has nothing to do with influencing our spirits, only through the flesh..." (JD 3:247). As Satan exercises his influence over our fleshy tabernacles, we will experience "feelings" which could be confusing if we are not careful.

While in Venezuela as a missionary, I met with a member who complained that he was having feelings that were troubling him. He would be impressed to do things that were partially correct, but not completely. For example, he felt that he must fast, but that it was acceptable to drink water while doing so. After some intense counseling and a priesthood blessing, this good brother was able to see that the spirit and feelings he was following were not right.

For the spiritual freshmen, how can we avoid embracing false feelings? Several guidelines might help. First, we must be worthy to receive the influence of the Holy Spirit. Unholy temples will be incapable of receiving the Lord's guidance and the feelings that accompany it. Second, true feelings will reflect the characteristics mentioned earlier: enlightenment, peace and joy. In contrast, we should shun any conflicting feelings of stupor or indifference. Third, the Spirit will always inspire us according to the revealed word of God and His anointed leaders. Joseph Smith taught: "I will inform you that it is contrary to the economy of God for any member of the Church, or any one, to receive instruction for those in authority, higher than themselves; therefore you will see the impropriety of giving heed to them" (*Teachings of the Prophet Joseph Smith*, p. 21). Unfortunately it is not uncommon to encounter individuals who consider themselves "privileged." They suppose they have a personal open conduit directly to the heavens through which they receive "special doctrines." Sometimes, their private revelations authorize them to ignore the counsel of their bishops and other priesthood or auxiliary leaders.

Last, we must not forget that the Lord may require patience as we seek a witness or His special direction. He does not operate on our time schedule. We may need to wait and continue our intense efforts to pierce the veil. Elder Boyd K. Packer observed:

> It is good to learn when you are young that spiritual things cannot be forced.
>
> Sometimes you may struggle with a problem and not get an answer. What could be wrong?
>
> It may be that you are not doing anything wrong. It may be that you have not done the right things long enough. Remember, you cannot force spiritual things.
>
> Sometimes we are confused simply because we won't take no for an answer (*That All May Be Edified*, p. 13).

Through time and experience we come to readily recognize the promptings of the Still Small Voice. His voice doesn't necessarily become louder, only clearer.

STEP FOUR: TRUSTING THE WITNESS

The witnesses we receive from our Heavenly Father concerning the truths we desire to discern may enter our hearts with different amounts of force. Occasionally, the influence of the Holy Ghost will give an almost overpowering witness which will instantaneously "burn" false beliefs out of our hearts, causing us to be "born again" and instantly transform our lives. The Nephites and others have experienced this (see Mosiah 4 and 5). Yet these occurrences are relatively rare.

At the other end of the spectrum, from an overwhelming witness, we identify a much simpler and subtle confirmation. It may be inadequately described as an assurance, a warm feeling, a gentle conviction, a quiet understanding which envelopes us. As our efforts reach up through the veil to God, He responds through the Holy Spirit. Elder Packer has stated: "The Spirit does not get our attention by shouting or shaking us with a heavy hand. Rather it whispers. It caresses so gently that if we are preoccupied we may not feel it at all" ("The Candle of the Lord," *Ensign*, Jan. 1983, p. 53).

Regardless of the type of witness we receive, we must acknowledge it for what it is and believe. Sometimes even after we have received an unmistakable "feeling" concerning the truthfulness of a doctrine, our belief may not be secure. We have so many different feelings, that in future moments we may struggle to recall the witness or to be firm in the conviction it reinforced. This phenomena is very common and serves to "shortcircuit" our efforts to thin the veil and increase our faith. It is one of Satan's most effective tools, among individuals who somehow muster a spiritual witness, that they barely understand.

Our responsibility requires us to continually remember the witness we have received. On one occasion the Lord reminded Oliver Cowdery concerning a witness he had received: "Verily, verily, I say unto you, if you desire a further witness, cast your mind upon the night that you cried unto me in your heart, that you might know concerning the truth of these things. Did I not speak peace to your mind concerning the matter? What greater witness can you have than from God? And now, behold, you have received a witness; for if I have told you things which no man knoweth have you not received a witness?" (D&C 6:22-24). The Lord could have sent a new witness or a duplicate of the previous, but He did not. He required Oliver to remember the witness he had already received. Later, the Lord needed to again remind Oliver Cowdery concerning the spiritual manifestations he had received: "Behold, I have manifested unto you, by my Spirit in many instances, that the things which you have written are true; wherefore you know that they are true" (D&C 18:2). Perhaps the Lord will repeatedly manifest truth to us, but at some point He expects us to believe and stop making the same requests.

Believing the spiritual guidance we receive requires us to trust it. Heavenly Father saw the need to remind Hyrum Smith to do just that: "And now, verily, verily, I say unto thee, put your trust in that Spirit which leadeth to do good—yea, to do justly, to walk humbly, to judge righteously; and this is my Spirit" (D&C 11:12). In answer to Hyrum's apparent concern or vacillation regarding the spiritual witness he had received, the Lord encouraged him to "trust in that Spirit." So too must we. His peace and Spirit can always be with us (D&C 20:79), but it would be unreasonable to require the Lord to repeatedly witness to us concerning a particular truth. He may answer prayers with a new spiritual confirmation, but more often He will expect us to do as Hyrum was admonished—that is, to trust in the witness we have already been sent and cultivate it so our beliefs and lives will change.

The Process

President Spencer W. Kimball explained it this way: "The Lord is eager to see their first awakening desires and their beginning efforts to penetrate the darkness. Having granted freedom of decision, he must permit man to grope his way until he reaches for the light. But when men begin to hunger, when arms begin to reach, when knees begin to bend and voices become articulate, then and not until then does the Father push back the horizons, draw back the veil and make it possible for men to emerge from dim, uncertain stumbling to sureness in the brilliance of the heavenly light" (*The Teachings of Spencer W. Kimball,* p. 423). Elder George Q. Cannon observed: "Our faith may be small in the beginning, but if we cultivate it, it will grow; if we do not it will die out, noxious weeds will spring up and choke it. But if we exercise it as we should, the veil of darkness that separates us from God, and which prevents us comprehending the things of His kingdom, will grow thinner and thinner, until we see with great distinctness and clearness the purposes of God our Heavenly Father, and comprehend them as He designs we should, and carry them out in our lives" (JD 13:373).

FAITH—"REACHINGS" AND RESULTS

These four steps result in new beliefs being formed within us. This is faith. However, the word "faith" may still seem confusing to some because it can refer different parts of the process. Great faith is found when people earnestly engage in step number two—*great reachings*. Still, great faith is found in relation to step three when *great spiritual witnesses* are sent from heaven. Additionally, great faith is manifest any time our efforts lead to *firm convictions* and trusting in the Lord.

Great "Reachings" Equal Great Faith

One example of great "reachings" may be identified in the Book of Alma. The father of King Lamoni met a missionary from Zarahemla named Aaron who taught him the gospel: "And Aaron did expound unto him the scriptures from the creation of Adam, laying the fall of man before him, and their carnal state and also the plan of redemption, which was prepared from the foundation of the world, through Christ" (Alma 22:13).

After this brief *introduction* to the plan of salvation, the King asked Aaron, "What shall I do that I may have this eternal life of which thou hast spoken? Yea, what shall I do that I may be born of God, having this wicked spirit rooted out of my breast, and receive His Spirit, that I may be filled with joy, that I may not be cast off at the last day? Behold, said he, I will give up all that I possess, yea, I will forsake my kingdom, that I may receive this great joy" (Alma 22:15).

At this point the King's behavior reflects an intense

desire (intense "reachings") to know concerning the teachings he had received and we would probably conclude that
he was exercising *great faith*. In response, Aaron told him
what more he must do: "If thou desirest this thing, if thou
wilt bow down before God, yea, if thou wilt repent of all thy
sins, and will bow down before God, and call on His name
in faith, believing that ye shall receive, then shalt thou
receive the hope which thou desirest" (Alma 22:16). The
King again demonstrated his *desire* (and faith) and
complied with the directive: "And it came to pass that when
Aaron had said these words, the King did bow down before
the Lord, upon his knees; yea, even he did prostrate himself
upon the earth, and cried mightily, saying: O God, Aaron
hath told me that there is a God; and if there is a God, and
if thou art God, wilt thou make thyself known unto me, and
I will give away all my sins to know thee, and that I may be
raised from the dead, and be saved at the last day" (Alma
22:17-18). In reply, the King received an undeniable
witness which caused him to be struck "as if he were dead."
After he awoke, he *trusted* the witness, allowing his new
beliefs to govern his actions. He exercised great faith and
his life was changed.

Great Spiritual Witnesses Equals Great Faith

Another form of great faith is found in individuals who have already reached *and* embraced the truths he or she was reaching for. Such individuals have already expended the energy required, the righteousness, the fasting, praying, scripture study and worship to enable them to receive multiple witnesses through the veil concerning eternal principles and doctrines. The results of their reachings provide evidence of great faith.

These people go about their daily duties with a calm conviction concerning eternal truths they cannot see. Those truths govern their lives. Their lives become living monuments to the truths located outside the veil. Over time, additional successful reachings (i.e. faith) provide further witnesses which expand these monuments into kingdoms.

4

Piercing the Veil

Learning about the veil helps us not only *reach* through it but could, if God wills, allow us to escape its effects all together. President Joseph F. Smith explained: "Sometimes the Lord expands our vision from this point of view and this side of the veil, that we feel and seem to realize that we can look beyond the thin veil which separates us from that other sphere" (*Gospel Doctrine,* p. 430). Brigham Young taught: "[T]he veil begins to be thinner, and will be withdrawn for us, if we are faithful. The work that God has commenced in this our day is calculated to remove the veil of the covering from all the face of the earth, that all flesh may see His glory together" (JD 8:114).

John Taylor observed, "We can have a portion of that Spirit by which we can draw back the veil of eternity and comprehend the designs of God that have been hidden up for generations past and gone. We can go back to our former existence and contemplate the designs of God in the formation of this earth and all things that pertain to it;

unravel its destiny and the designs of God in relation to our past, present, and future existence" (*The Gospel Kingdom*, p. 111).

OBTAINING A "PERFECT KNOWLEDGE"

Above and beyond the knowledge we gain through faith is what Alma calls receiving a "perfect knowledge." He explains that once a "perfect knowledge" is achieved, faith is no longer present regarding that particular thing (Alma 32:21, 29). A "perfect knowledge" involves a witness which seems to include our physical senses as well as "feelings" from the Holy Spirit.

The Brother of Jared received this "perfect knowledge." He built barges to cross the ocean using the directions given him from the Lord. After their completion, he discovered the deep darkness inside. He asked the Lord to touch sixteen small stones which he had molten out of rock, that they might provide light for the journey across the ocean. The premortal Jesus complied with his request and even showed Himself to the brother of Jared:

> [T]he Lord showed Himself unto him, and said: Because thou knowest these things ye are redeemed from the fall; therefore ye are brought back into my presence; therefore I show myself unto you...
>
> And because of the knowledge of this man he could not be kept from beholding within the veil; and he saw the finger of Jesus, which, when he saw, he fell with fear; for he knew that it was the finger of the Lord; and *he had faith no longer, for he knew, nothing doubting.*
>
> Wherefore, having this *perfect knowledge* of God, he could not be kept from within the veil; therefore he saw

Jesus; and he did minister unto him (Ether 3:13, 19-20; italics added).

Through the Spirit, the Brother of Jared seemed to see with his eyes and hear with his ears as the veil was rent. His witness apparently transcended the "feelings" communicated alone into our hearts and minds by the Holy Spirit. The key to a "perfect knowledge" seems to require *both* the undeniable witness of the Holy Spirit *and* an experience which seems to involve the physical senses.

However, a strictly physical manifestation to our senses without the spiritual "feelings" given by the Holy Spirit is practically useless in creating faith. Brigham Young explained:

> The eloquence of angels never can convince any person that God lives and makes truth the habitation of His throne, independent of that eloquence being clothed with the power of the Holy Ghost; in the absence of this, it would be a combination of useless sounds. What is it that convinces man? It is the influence of the Almighty, enlightening his mind, giving instruction to the understanding, when that which inhabits this body, that which came from the regions of Glory, is enlightened by the influence, power and Spirit of the Father of Light, it swallows up the organization which pertains to this world. Many evil men have seen miracles with their eyes and yet have easily denied the witness. Jesus healed the sick and even raised the dead, but many of the observers were unimpressed and even sought to take His life (*Discourses of Brigham Young*, p. 34).

As noted above, the Jews who rejected Christ viewed with their eyes the miraculous events Christ wrought.

Nevertheless, their complete ignorance of the workings of the Holy Spirit left them destitute of a spiritual witness. Marooned upon the island of their own temporal experience, they had long rejected attempts by the Holy Spirit to bring them to the port of all truth and spiritual convictions. They were clearly "past feeling" (Eph. 4:19). They would not receive the spiritual "feelings" which could magnify an impressive miracle into a life-transforming event.

Concerning such knowledge, President Spencer W. Kimball once counseled:

> Many, in former days and in latter days, have given their lives for their faith. You can know so surely that this is the divine truth that you also would give your life, your profession, or your all or any part of it for your testimony. If you do not receive this assurance, this testimony, it is your fault. The Lord is most anxious to give it to you through the Holy Ghost when you have really humbled yourself and paid the price in reaching, fasting, praying, studying, pondering, and cleansing and purging. You have spent years of intense study to gain your professional knowledge. Half as much devotion to your spiritual knowledge with the other requisites would have made your faith invincible, and you would not now be floundering (*Teachings of Spencer W. Kimball*, p. 64).

Transcending Sight and Sound

We may wonder concerning the actual mechanics of the process through which the veil might be removed as with the brother of Jared and others. The scriptures do not explain the sequence outright, but they give many examples from which we may learn.

When a portion of the veil is fully rent, the recipient of the divine communication appears to receive some form of sensory input which impresses the mind. It seems to transcend our physical senses but is often described as involving sight and even hearing in some way. The Lord seems to have alluded to this process: "And the day cometh that you shall hear my voice and see me, and know that I am" (D&C 50:45).

JOSEPH SMITH AND OLIVER COWDERY
The veil was taken from our minds, and the *eyes* of our understanding were opened... (D&C 110:1).

THE BROTHER OF JARED
[T]he veil was taken from off the *eyes*... (Ether 3:6).

JOSEPH SMITH AND SIDNEY RIGDON
By the power of the Spirit our *eyes* were opened and our understandings were enlightened, so as to *see* and understand the things of God... (D&C 76:12).

JOSEPH SMITH:
The heavens were opened upon us...whether in the body or out I cannot tell... (D&C 137:1).

JOSEPH F. SMITH:

[T]he *eyes* of my understanding were opened, and the Spirit of the Lord rested upon me... (D&C 138:11).

PAUL

[W]hether in the body, I cannot tell; or whether out of the body, I cannot tell... (2 Cor. 12:2).

JOHN THE REVELATOR

I was in the Spirit on the Lord's day, and *heard* behind me a great voice, as of a trumpet... (Revelation 1:10).

MOSES

[C]aught up into an exceedingly high mountain... and the glory of God was upon [him]... [M]ine own *eyes* have beheld God; but not my natural, but my spiritual eyes, for my natural eyes could not have beheld (Moses 1:1-2, 11).

LEHI

Being thus overcome with the Spirit, he was carried away in a vision, even that he *saw* the heavens open... (1 Ne. 1:8).

NEPHI

I was caught away in the Spirit of the Lord, yea, into an exceedingly high mountain, which I never had before seen, and upon which I never had before set my foot.... And mine *eyes*... beheld great things, yea, even too great for man (1 Ne. 11:1, 2 Ne. 4:25).

ABRAHAM

[T]he Lord had *shown* unto me... (Abr. 3:23).

ENOCH:
[T]he Lord *showed* unto [him]... (Moses 7:21)

Concerning John the Revelator, Joseph Smith taught that he "had the curtains of heaven withdrawn, and by vision *looked* through the dark vista of future ages, and contemplated events that should transpire throughout every subsequent period of time, until the final winding up scene" that "he *gazed* upon the glories of the eternal world, saw an innumerable company of angels and heard the voice of God" (*Teachings of the Prophet Joseph Smith*, p. 247; italics added). Again it is implied that sight and sound were employed in some transcendent manner. On another occasion, the Prophet counseled: "God has so ordained that when He has communicated, no vision is to be taken but what you see by the *seeing of the eye*, or what you hear by the *hearing of the ear*. When you see a vision, pray for the interpretation; if you get not this, shut it up; there must be certainty in this matter. An open vision will manifest that which is more important" (*Teachings of the Prophet Joseph Smith*, p. 161; emphasis added).

Removing the Veil Exposes New Knowledge

Specific portions of the veil can vanish as individuals are privileged to view different aspects of eternity. However, veil-rending experiences differ in important ways. If we review the volume of knowledge imparted as the veil is thinned, we discover an entire spectrum seems to exist. At one end we find instances where the veil is removed, but little information is received. Paul admits that it is possible to entertain angels "unaware" of their identity (Hebrews 13:2).

Consider Laman and Lemuel who viewed an angel (1 Nephi 3:29-31). He instructed them to stop smiting their brother (Nephi) and gave a few other elements of instruction. Overall however, comparatively little knowledge seems to have been shared and even that which was given was quickly disbelieved by both Laman and Lemuel.

At the other end of the spectrum, we find prophets who experienced situations where a great portion of the veil was rent. As the glory of the Lord enveloped them, they were able to "see" and otherwise comprehend great volumes of information.

MOSES

And it came to pass that Moses looked, and beheld the world upon which he was created; and *Moses beheld the world and the ends thereof, and all the children of men which are, and which were created*; of the same he greatly marveled and wondered (Moses 1:8).

Moses cast his eyes and *beheld the earth, yea, even all of it; and there was not a particle of it which he did not behold*, discerning it by the spirit of God.

And he beheld also the inhabitants thereof, and there was not a soul which he beheld not; and he discerned them by the Spirit of God; and their numbers were great, even numberless as the sand upon the sea shore.

And he beheld many lands; and each land was called earth, and there were inhabitants on the face thereof (Moses 1:27-29).

Abraham

Thus I, Abraham, talked with the Lord, face to face, as one man talketh with another; and He told me of the works which His hands had made;

And He said unto me: My son, my son (and His hand was stretched out), behold I will show you all these. And He put His hand upon mine eyes, and *I saw those things which His hands had made, which were many; and they multiplied before mine eyes, and I could not see the end thereof* (Abraham 3:11-12).

Enoch

And it came to pass that the Lord showed unto Enoch *all the inhabitants of the earth* (Moses 7:21).

The Brother of Jared

And when the Lord had said these words, He showed unto the brother of Jared *all the inhabitants of the earth which had been, and also all that would be; and He withheld them not from his sight, even unto the ends of the earth* (Ether 3:25).

Other scriptures include accounts which demonstrate a similar "panoramic" view which is revealed as a part of the veil is removed. Joseph Smith certainly experienced this (D&C 76 and 88). John the Revelator gave us the Book of Revelations. Prophets Ezekiel and Joel viewed tremendous visions.

Physical Effects of Removing the Veil

Admittedly the incidents we are told about where the veil is rent during mortality are few. Yet they do occur and when they do, they commonly remove physical strength from the mortal recipient. After receiving the First Vision, Joseph related that "I found myself lying on my back, looking up into heaven. When the light had departed, *I had no strength...*" (JSH 1:20). Moses' experience was similar:

> And the presence of God withdrew from Moses, that His glory was not upon Moses; and Moses was left unto himself. And as he was left unto himself, he fell unto the earth.
> And it came to pass that it was for the space of many hours before Moses did again receive his natural strength like unto man; and he said unto himself: Now, for this cause I know that man is nothing... (Moses 1:9-10).

In this dispensation a similar incident occurred after reception of Section 76 of the Doctrine and Covenants by Joseph Smith and Sidney Rigdon. The account as recorded in the *Juvenile Instructor,* May 15th, 1892, reads:

> Joseph would, at intervals, say: "What do I see?" Then he would relate what he had seen or what he was looking at. Then Sidney replied, "I see the same." Presently Sidney would say, "What do I see?" and would repeat what he had seen or was seeing, and Joseph would reply, "I see the same." This manner of conversation was repeated at short intervals to the end of the vision, and during the whole time not a word was spoken by any other person. Not a sound nor motion made by anyone but Joseph and Sidney, and it seemed to me that they

never moved a joint or limb during the time I was there, which I think was over an hour, and to the end of the vision. Joseph sat firmly and calmly all the time in the midst of a magnificent glory, but *Sidney sat limp and pale, apparently as limber as a rag, observing which Joseph remarked, smilingly, "Sidney is not used to it as I am"* (italics added).

Other accounts exist suggesting that some theophanies may be "energizing" in that the participants feel more strength after than they did before.

THE PROMISE IS TO US

While in mortality it is difficult to understand these visions. We may wonder, "How can any being behold 'the ends of the earth' and 'the inhabitants thereof'?" Our mortal minds may be incapable of understanding the process, but we know that such images and knowledge have been given to righteous, though imperfect, mortals in the past. The Lord has promised it to us today: "For he that diligently seeketh shall find; and the mysteries of God shall be unfolded unto them, by the power of the Holy Ghost, as well in these times as in times of old, and as well in times of old as in times to come; wherefore, the course of the Lord is one eternal round" (1 Nephi 10:19). "If thou shalt ask, thou shalt receive revelation upon revelation, knowledge upon knowledge, that thou mayest know the mysteries and peaceable things—that which bringeth joy, that which bringeth life eternal" (D&C 42:61).

The Lord may have given us a pattern for such communications in the experiences of Moses, Abraham, Enoch and the Brother of Jared (see D&C 52:14). If so, we may assume that if the veil was rent for some holy man or woman today, that person might be privileged to view some of the same things which they saw. The following account from the *History of the Church* contains an interesting description of the very first conference of the church where part of the veil was removed for several members:

Much exhortation and instruction was given, and the Holy Ghost was poured out upon us in a miraculous manner—many of our number prophesied, whilst others had the heavens opened to their view, and were so overcome that we had to lay them on beds or other convenient places; among the rest was Brother Newel Knight, who had to be placed on a bed, being unable to help himself. By his own account of the transaction, he could not understand why we should lay him on the bed, as he felt no sense of weakness. He felt his heart filled with love, with glory, and pleasure unspeakable, and could discern all that was going on in the room; when all of a sudden a vision of the future burst upon him. He saw there represented the great work which through my instrumentality was yet to be accomplished. *He saw heaven opened, and beheld the Lord Jesus Christ, seated at the right hand of the majesty on high, and had it made plain to his understanding that the time would come when he would be admitted into His presence to enjoy His society for ever and ever.* When their bodily strength was restored to these brethren, they shouted hosannas to God and the Lamb, and rehearsed the glorious things which they had seen and felt, whilst they were yet in the spirit.

Such scenes as these were calculated to inspire our hearts with joy unspeakable, and fill us with awe and reverence for that Almighty Being, by whose grace we had been called to be instrumental in bringing about, for the children of men, the enjoyment of such glorious blessings as were now at this time poured out upon us. To find ourselves engaged in the very same order of things as observed by the holy Apostles of old; to realize the importance and solemnity of such proceedings; and *to witness and feel with our own natural senses,* the like glorious manifestations of the powers of the priesthood, the gifts and blessings of the Holy Ghost, and the goodness and condescension of a merciful God unto such as obey the everlasting Gospel of our Lord Jesus Christ, combined to create within us sensations of rapturous gratitude, and inspire us with fresh zeal and energy in the cause of truth (1:84-86; italics added).

This account also suggests that the veil-rending incident experienced by these worthy men and women truly involved their "own natural senses." They were overcome with the Spirit allowing them to suddenly detect and comprehend eternity on a level previously unknown to them.

Brigham Young believed we can all enjoy veil-rending experiences during mortality:

Can mortal beings live so that they are worthy of the society of angels? I can answer the question for myself—I believe that they can; I am sure that they can. But in doing this, they must subdue the sin that is within themselves, correct every influence that arises within their own hearts that is opposed to the sanctifying influences of the grace of God, and purify themselves by their faith and by their conduct, so that they are worthy. Then they are prepared for the society of angels. To be Saints indeed requires every wrong influence that is within them, as individuals, to be subdued, until every evil desire is eradicated, and every feeling of their hearts is brought into subjection to the will of Christ (*Discourses of Brigham Young*, p. 91).

Learning of Eternity

When eternity is experienced, mortals often encounter things they never anticipated or otherwise conceived. Apparently eternity is filled with wonderful realities which are quite foreign to this telestial sphere and to the thoughts of mortal beings. Paul observed: "Eye hath not seen, nor ear heard, neither have entered into the heart of man, the things which God hath prepared for them that love Him" (1 Corinthians 2:9). Likewise, Moses confronted things he "never had supposed" (Moses 1:10) in his visions.

These transcending eternal truths may easily exceed our ability to adequately write or speak of them. Joseph Smith once prayed that the veil might be lifted from his mind allowing him and those that were with him to learn more rapidly than our language and the published word permits:

> Oh, Lord, when will the time come when [we] shall behold the day that we may stand together and gaze upon eternal wisdom engraven upon the heavens, while the majesty of our God holdeth up the dark curtain until we may read the round of eternity, to the fullness and satisfaction of our immortal souls? Oh, Lord, deliver us in due time from the little, narrow prison, almost as it were, total darkness of paper, pen and ink;—and a crooked, broken, scattered and imperfect language (*History of the Church* 1:299).

It appears that beyond the veil it is much easier to share feelings and knowledge. Brigham Young taught:

I long for the time that a point of the finger, or motion of the hand, will express every idea without utterance. *When a man is full of the light of eternity, then the eye is not the only medium through which he sees, his ear is not the only medium by which he hears, nor the brain the only means by which he understands.* When the whole body is full of the Holy Ghost, he can see behind him with as much ease, without turning his head, as he can see before him. If you have not that experience, you ought to have. It is not the optic nerve alone that gives the knowledge of surrounding objects to the mind, but it is that which God has placed in man—a system of intelligence that attracts knowledge, as light cleaves to light, intelligence to intelligence, and truth to truth. It is this which lays in man a proper foundation for all education (*Discourses of Brigham Young*, p. 257; italics added).

GOD AWAITS AT THE VEIL

Experiences where the veil is thinned or removed are available to all worthy individuals. They are not restricted to the male gender or to ordained Church leaders. Alma advised: "And now, behold, I say unto you, and I would that ye should remember, that God is merciful unto all who believe on His name; therefore He desireth, in the first place, that ye should believe, yea, even on His word. And now, He imparteth His word by angels unto men, yea, not only men but women also. Now this is not all; little children do have words given unto them many times, which confound the wise and the learned" (Alma 32:22-23).

Veil-rending experiences can be ours. The scriptures teach that we should, "seek the face of the Lord always" (D&C 101:38). President James E. Faust observed: "I would surmise that all who are members of this great Church have a desire to see the face of the Savior. *This is an available blessing* for he has said, 'Verily, thus saith the Lord: It shall come to pass that every soul who forsaketh his sins and cometh unto me, and calleth on my name, and obeyeth my voice, and keepeth my commandments, shall see my face and know that I am' (D&C 93:1)" (*Ensign*, Aug. 1999, pp. 4-5; italics added). Similar promises are found in D&C 88:68 and 67:10.

Elder Howard W. Hunter explained: "The supreme achievement of life is to find God and to know that He lives. Like any other worthy accomplishment, this can only be obtained by those who will believe and have faith in that which at first may not be apparent. This is the road to exaltation" (*The Teachings of Howard W. Hunter*, p. 28). President Kimball explained: "The ultimate and greatest of all knowledge, then, is to know God and His program for our exaltation. *We may know Him by sight, by sound, by feeling.* While relatively few ever do really know Him, everyone may know Him, not only prophets..." (*Teachings of Spencer W. Kimball*, p. 7; italics added).

Having reviewed the wonderful vision received by the brother of Jared, Elder Jeffrey R. Holland explained that: "Ordinary individuals with ordinary challenges could rend the veil of unbelief and enter the realms of eternity. And Christ, who was prepared from the foundation of the world to redeem His people, would be standing at the edge of that veil to usher the believer through" (*Nurturing Faith Through the Book of Mormon*, p. 24).

The question remains whether we are ready to expend the effort to humbly kneel and tug at the veil. "Behold, I stand at the door, and knock: if any man hear my voice, and open the door, I will come in to him, and will sup with him, and he with me" (Revelation 3:20). In this verse, the door is a metaphor but the veil is real and so is the promise.

5

Satan and the Veil

Forfeiting our premortal memories and losing contact with Heavenly Father and the Spirit World are probably not the most significant influences the veil thrusts upon us. Both are temporary for the righteous. Possibly its greatest influence is manifested as it hides the eternal consequences of sin. It thereby conceals eternal compromises and eternal dangers.

THE VEIL HIDES ETERNAL CONSEQUENCES

It seems that the only way Heavenly Father could guarantee that we would have unfettered agency during mortality was to impose a veil upon us at birth.

Agency and the Veil

God gave us our agency in the premortal world. It is a great gift. President David O. McKay explained: "Next to the bestowal of life itself, the right to direct that life is God's greatest gift to man.... It is inherent in the spirit of man. It is a divine gift to every normal being" (*Gospel Ideals*, p. 299). As premortal spirits we were able to make choices and to exercise our free agency. We enjoyed freedom doing the things that a spirit body could do. One exception existed for us: We could not disobey the Father without consequence. We could disobey. We could ignore Heavenly Father's directives in the premortal world. And we all did in some degree except for Jesus Christ. But we could not do it without consequence, not without repercussion. For one-third of the spirits, their premortal wickedness was sufficient to warrant a consequence of being cast out of Heavenly Father's presence forever.

Having passed through the veil to arrive here on earth, we retain this exceptional gift of agency. Nephi explained that because of Christ's atonement: "They have become free forever, knowing good from evil; to act for themselves and not to be acted upon..." (2 Nephi 2:26).

The Veil Creates an Illusion

Being surrounded by the veil on earth conceals the one limitation upon our agency which we understood in the premortal world. Here, the veil generates the illusion that we can sin without eternal consequence. It enables us to temporarily embrace the "big lie"—that *sin is desirable*. President Wilford Woodruff observed:

There is a veil between man and eternal things; if that veil was taken away and we were able to see eternal things as they are before the Lord, no man would be tried with regard to gold, silver or this world's goods, and no man, on their account, would be unwilling to let the Lord control him. But here we have an agency, and we are in a probation, and there is a veil between us and eternal things, between us and our Heavenly Father and the spirit world; and this for a wise and proper purpose in the Lord our God, to prove whether the children of men will abide in His law or not in the situation in which they are placed here (JD 17:71).

Within the shadow of the veil, disobedience may appear acceptable or even enjoyable. Figuratively, the veil places us in eternal "blinders." Blinders prevent a horse from seeing the dangers which may exist on either side of him as he treads along. They permit the horse to proceed on an otherwise dangerous course, completely unaware of even life-threatening risks that may be around him. Equally, the veil places blinders on us regarding our sins. By shutting out the eternal realities around us, we are free to focus upon the contracted view of sin which may make it appear desirable. Its inherent eternal ugliness is more easily ignored. This narrow view allows the perceived benefits of our imperfections to appear to outweigh the liabilities they bring. The veil may create a cozy isolated "comfort zone" within our minds where the seeds of selected flawed behaviors can intermittently sprout or even flourish.

Eternal Consequences Persist Unseen

It is so easy to ignore the eternal ramifications of sin while living within the veil. Sometimes we may think that we are aware of all of the consequences when in fact the greater perils our sins produce actually exist beyond the veil in eternity. The Lord warned: "For all flesh is corrupted before me; and the powers of darkness prevail upon the earth, among the children of men, *in the presence of all the hosts of heaven–Which causeth silence to reign, and all eternity is pained,* and the angels are waiting the great command to reap down the earth, to gather the tares that they may be burned" (D&C 38:11-12; italics added).

I recall one day when I was attending high school, a friend of mine discovered that if you would vigorously shake a cable supporting a power pole which was located next to the gymnasium, the power lines above would eventually come close enough to each other to send out a glorious display of sparks. He thought it was great fun. After shaking the wire for a while, he noticed that the sparks quit. He didn't think too much of it until he went inside for his next class to learn that the electricity was out throughout the entire school. Also, he was unaware that several miles away at the power plant, two generators had been burned up which required several thousand dollars to rewire. My friend had a great time shaking the wire. Afterwards he quickly became aware of some of the consequences of his behavior as he entered the darkened school building. Yet, he had created even greater problems beyond his ability to immediately discern by burning up the generators. Sin is like that. We may feel we are having a good time while engaged in it. But we cannot easily detect how our mortal sins are, even at that moment, destroying eternal possibilities and compromising our eternal destinies.

The Veil Hides the Purpose of Mortality

Besides concealing the way sin stunts our celestial growth, the veil permits a more subtle wickedness. It hides the purpose of mortality. Our brief sojourn upon this earth is immensely important to our eternal progression. The veil conceals the work we were sent here to do. With the veil firmly in place, it is easy to use our time and resources pursuing things of little eternal significance.

SATAN AND THE VEIL

A second factor amplifies our ability to sin while living in the veil. Lucifer and his followers are here and have been granted the power to tempt us (D&C 29:39). They are constantly trying to entice earth's inhabitants to break God's laws. Brigham Young explained: "[T]he very great majority prefer to do good rather than to do evil, and would pursue a correct course, were it not for the evil power that subjects them to its sway" (*Discourses of Brigham Young*, p. 67).

The adversary will exploit all of the advantages the veil provides him. He knows that within its shadow he can successfully decorate various forms of evil so they appear attractive, if not enchanting. He knows that a faithless generation is easily fooled because they will not seek to pierce the veil to discover the sham he constantly perpetrates. "Satan seeketh to turn their hearts away from the truth, that they become blinded and understand not the things which are prepared for them" (D&C 78:10).

Perhaps Satan even takes credit for the presence of the veil. The prophet Enoch, "beheld Satan; and he had a great chain in his hand, and it veiled the whole face of the earth with darkness; and he looked up and laughed, and his angels rejoiced" (Moses 7:26).

President Wilford Woodruff summed it up by saying: "Lucifer was cast down to the earth with the third part of the hosts of heaven, and they have dwelt here until today. They remain here yet; and they have had their effect upon the hearts and minds and lives of the children of men for nearly six thousand years—from the time that man was cast out of the Garden of Eden into the cold and dreary world" (*The Discourses of Wilford Woodruff*, p. 241).

President George Q. Cannon, a member of the First Presidency at the turn of the century observed:

> Now there is a veil between us and our Father, and we are left to ourselves, to a certain extent. We are left to be governed by the influences that we invite, and there are any number of evil influences around us, whispering into our ears and hearts all manner of things. If we will open our hearts to receive them or allow them to enter our hearts, we will think evil of our brethren and of our sisters; we will have malice towards them; we will envy them; and we will say bad things about them. God will test us in all this" (*Gospel Truth,* p. 7).

A Pattern Revealed As Satan Tempts the Savior

It is possible that the confrontation between Lucifer and Jesus Christ illustrates Satan's most tempting enticements.

Perhaps it reveals the Adversary's most advanced methods which he continues to implement to spread darkness throughout the world.

Undoubtedly, Satan and his followers prepared for centuries, if not millennia for that singular occasion to tempt Jesus. They knew that if they were successful, they could in one short incident, destroy Jesus' role in the Plan of Salvation. One wonders how many different approaches were considered and how much time was spent pondering the exact words that Lucifer was to use in his sole opportunity to tempt the Only Begotten Son of the Father? Who might Satan have chosen to assist him on the council or committee that he may have appointed to address the issue? What preparations were performed in the world of darkness in anticipation of that moment?

These inquiries underscore the value of carefully reviewing the questions Satan posed to Christ. Satan knew there would probably be no second chance for a similar confrontation with the Firstborn Son, so the adversary would need to choose the most inviting and enticing temptations he or any of his followers could concoct. To present Christ with anything less would diminish the possibility of success and assure the eternal damnation of all evil spirits. Hence, Satan was highly motivated to present Jesus the most tantalizing temptations possible. He had over 4,000 years of experience tempting mortals and even longer seducing premortal spirits which must have helped him as he selected his enticements.

> Then Jesus was led up of the Spirit, into the wilderness, to be with God.
> And when He had fasted forty days and forty nights, and had communed with God, He was afterwards an

hungered, and was left to be tempted of the devil.

And when the tempter came to Him, he said, "*If thou be the Son of God, command that these stones be made bread.*"

But Jesus answered and said, "It is written, Man shall not live by bread alone, but by every word that proceedeth out of the mouth of God."

Then Jesus was taken up into the holy city, and the Spirit setteth Him on the pinnacle of the temple.

Then the devil came unto Him and said, "*If thou be the Son of God, cast thyself down, for it is written, He shall give His angels charge concerning thee, and in their hands they shall bear thee up, lest at any time thou dash thy foot against a stone.*"

Jesus said unto him, "It is written again, Thou shalt not tempt the Lord thy God."

And again, Jesus was in the Spirit, and it taketh Him up into an exceeding high mountain, and showeth Him *all the kingdoms of the world and the glory of them.*

And the devil came unto Him again, and said, All these things will I give unto thee, if thou wilt fall down and worship me.

Then said Jesus unto him, "Get thee hence, Satan"; for it is written, "Thou shalt worship the Lord thy God, and Him only shalt thou serve. Then the devil leaveth Him" (JST Matt. 4:1-10; italics added).

President David O. McKay made the following observations concerning the temptations presented the Savior:

When Satan said, "...command that these stones be made bread," (Matt. 4:3) he was appealing to the *appetite.* He knew that Jesus was hungry, that he was physically weak and thought that by pointing to those little limestones which resemble somewhat a Jewish loaf of bread, he could awaken a desire to eat. Failing in that, he received the divine word, "...Man shall not live by bread alone, but by every word that proceedeth out of the mouth of God" (Ibid., 4:4). Satan then tried him in another way. He dared him—an appeal to his *pride*, to his *vanity*...

But the Savior answered him in terms of scripture, "It is written again, Thou shalt not tempt the Lord thy God" (Matt. 4:7). What was the third? An appeal to his love of *power*, domain, *wealth*, "All these things [the kingdoms of the world and the glory thereof] will I give thee," said the tempter, "if thou wilt fall down and worship me" (Ibid., 4:9). "Get thee hence, Satan: for it is written, Thou shalt worship the Lord thy God, and Him only shalt thou serve" (Ibid., 4:10). *Now, nearly every temptation that comes to you and me comes in one of those forms.* Classify them, and you will find that under one of those three, nearly every given temptation that makes you and me spotted, ever so little maybe, comes to us as (1) a temptation of the appetite or passion; (2) a yielding to the pride and fashion or vanity of those alienated from the things of God; or (3) a desire for the riches of the world or power among men (*Gospel Ideals*, pp. 154–155; italics added).

Accordingly, Satan spreads darkness by enticing us to exploit (1) egotism, (2) materialism, and (3) physical appetites.

What if aliens were to fly to earth from a distant planet? If they visited America today, to watch our movies and television programs, read our books, magazines and newspapers, listen to our music, tune in our radios and view our billboards, if they were to eavesdrop into our conversations in our cars and at our places of business and observe our activities in our leisure hours, what would they identify as our guiding priorities? Would an alien conclude that the primary values of our society center around three things: bodily appetites (sex, food, aggression, drugs, etc.), egotistic endeavors (recognition, praise, money, power, etc.) and materialistic objects (money, homes, cars, boats, recreation, vacations, etc.)? If aliens would conclude this, what about angels? What about our Heavenly Father? Though we cannot see Him, He is well aware of our sins which seem camouflaged within the veil (Heb. 4:13).

PURSUING VANITY AND EGO

The veil hides the folly of pursuing vanity and ego. Ego might be defined as "An exaggerated sense of self-importance" (American Heritage Dictionary). The veil enhances our ability to express vanity and ego because it conceals our own inherent eternal insignificance. We are less than the dust of the earth (Hel. 12:7). It is only through the grace of God that we can be transformed into creatures of glory. We have no power of ourselves to do it. Within the veil we can exalt ourselves so that we honestly believe we are more important than other people. We can also embrace the notion that we don't need God or that He doesn't exist.

Premortal Vanity

As an undesirable personality trait, vanity was apparently present in the premortal world. Joseph Smith instructed: "Now, in this world, mankind are naturally selfish, ambitious and striving to excel one above another; yet some are willing to build up others as well as themselves. So in the other [premortal] world, there are a variety of spirits. Some seek to excel. And this was the case with

Lucifer when he fell. He sought for things which were unlawful. Hence he was sent down, and it is said he drew many away with him" (*Teachings of the Prophet Joseph Smith*, p. 297). We can only imagine the amount of vanity which motivated Satan to confront God the Father, a glorified celestial being, and even to rebel against His plan. We know that Satan had great authority in the premortal realm which undoubtedly enhanced his own visions of grandeur (D&C 76:25). But his knowledge and power were obviously inferior to God's. We are told that, "he knew not the mind of God" (Moses 4:6). Relying upon his own wisdom, he enticed the heavenly hosts to rebel with him. One-third exercised their agency to follow. Here on earth they all entice us to vanity and to expand our egos.

A preponderance of ego has the power to poison the relationship we should have with our Heavenly Father. While He is the Father of our spirits and loves us, He has sent us to earth with a commandment that we follow after Him and obey His word. Surrounded by the veil, we can easily forget or ignore Him. We can pursue things which the world values. The Lord warned: "That which is highly esteemed among men is abomination in the sight of God" (Luke 16:15). We can dispense with prayer, scripture study, and worship, believing that such are only for the weak and that without them we are strong. Characteristics of godliness are also spurned including meekness, humility, submissiveness, longsuffering and patience. It becomes easy to substitute selfishness, arrogance, vanity and pride.

Our eternal relationship with other human beings is one of spirit-siblings. The veil causes us to forget this important fact and sets the stage for egotistical individuals to climb to the top of the ladder of success figuratively by stepping on and over the bodies of other people. With the veil in place, we can more easily embrace Korihor's argument that: "Every man fared in this life according to the management of the creature; therefore every man prospered according to his genius, and that every man conquered according to his strength; and whatsoever a man did was no crime" (Alma 30:17). We may feel justified belittling others, the sick, the poor, the uneducated or any less fortunate than ourselves.

Sometimes manifestations of pride may be less obvious among Latter-day Saints. Yet, it is possible for a person to use his gospel knowledge or Church position to build his ego. We can "wear" our apparent spirituality, spiritual knowledge or Church calling as an ornament for all to see. We may convince ourselves that we sincerely desire to serve God unaware that our *desire for impact* within the ward (or stake) stems more from aspirations for the recognition of the members than the motivation to meekly assist.

PURSUING MATERIALISM

The world we live in is beautiful and the Lord intends for His Saints to derive joy and happiness from it. He told Joseph Smith:

[T]he fulness of the earth is yours, the beasts of the field and the fowls of the air, and that which climbeth upon the trees and walketh upon the earth;

Yea, and the herb, and the good things which come of the earth, whether for food or for raiment, or for houses, or for barns, or for orchards, or for gardens, or for vineyards;

Yea, all things which come of the earth, in the season thereof, are made for the benefit and the use of man, both to please the eye and to gladden the heart;

Yea, for food and for raiment, for taste and for smell, to strengthen the body and to enliven the soul.

And it pleaseth God that He hath given all these things unto man; for unto this end were they made to be used, with judgment, not to excess, neither by extortion" (D&C 59:16-20).

However, living within the veil we can easily center our lives upon material things. Jesus warned against such: "Take heed, and beware of covetousness: for a man's life consisteth not in the abundance of the things which he possesseth" (Luke 12:15). Then He shared the following story:

X   The ground of a certain rich man brought forth plentifully:

And he thought within himself, saying, What shall I do, because I have no room where to bestow my fruits?

And he said, This will I do: I will pull down my barns, and build greater; and there will I bestow all my fruits and my goods.

And I will say to my soul, Soul, thou hast much goods laid up for many years; take thine ease, eat, drink, and be merry.

But God said unto him, Thou fool, this night thy soul shall be required of thee: then whose shall those things be, which thou hast provided? (Luke 12:16-20)

This rich man seems to have focused his life upon his material goods. It appears that he forgot that at any instant he could be forced to leave his possessions and be propelled through the veil of death to a new realm of existence. When the Lord said: "This night thy soul shall be required of thee," the veil which had been so incredibly thick for him became a memory. It is a moment which will occur in each of our lives. At the time we pass through the veil of death, we will receive little comfort from the material possessions we may have accumulated on earth.

Needs and Wants

In our quest for material things, the Lord seems to allow the righteous to go beyond acquiring the bare essentials. It appears we may be justified occasionally to pursue not only "needs" but selected "wants" as well (see D&C 51:3,8). The material things found upon this earth have been provided for us as the "means" to allow us to accomplish the things required for exaltation. However, within the confines of the veil, the acquisition of material things can easily become our primary goal in life, not the "means" but the "ends" of our work here on earth. Brigham Young taught:

> A man or a woman who places the wealth of this world and the things of time in the scales against the things of God and the wisdom of eternity, has no eyes to see, no ears to hear, no heart to understand. What are riches for? For blessings, to do good. Then let us dispense that which the Lord gives us to the best possible use, for the building up of His Kingdom, for the promotion of the truth on the earth, that we may see and enjoy the blessings of the Zion of God here upon this earth. I look around among the world of mankind and see them grabbing, scrambling, contending, and every one seeking to aggrandize himself, and to accomplish his own individual purposes, passing the community by, walking upon the heads of his neighbors—all are seeking, planning, contriving in their wakeful hours, and when asleep dreaming, "How can I get

the advantage of my neighbor? How can I spoil him, that I may ascend the ladder of fame?" This is entirely a mistaken idea (*Discourses of Brigham Young*, p. 307).

The pursuit of wealth can also enhance egotistical demonstrations. Sometimes our houses, cars, clothes and jewelry might seem to advertise the idea that "The owner of this item has lots of money." Sometimes it could reflect "I've got more money than you do."

The Gift of Time

On earth we have our agency and God's gift of time. "I have told you many times," President Brigham Young said, "the property which we inherit from our Heavenly Father is our *time*, and the power to choose in the disposition of the same. This is the real capital that is bequeathed unto us by our Heavenly Father" (JD 18:354; emphasis added). God expects us to use our time to exalt ourselves and others by following His commandments. Nonetheless, the veil effectively conceals His expectations.

Alternatives exist. We can utilize our time seeking to acquire more material things or enjoying the acquisitions directly. We may aspire to the saying, "He who dies with the most toys wins!" It is sometimes difficult to leave the "gold standard" where we exchange a majority of our time for money and material things. However, at some point we might realize that we have already obtained sufficient material resources to meet our needs and beyond. Regardless, we may all benefit by exchanging the "gold standard" for a "God standard" where we consciously exchange our time, not for material wealth, but for the things of God. The things of God originate outside the veil but will always require our *time* to capture them.

The Lord has warned: "[The inhabitants of the earth] seek not the Lord to establish his righteousness, but every man walketh in his own way, and after the image of his own god, whose image is in the likeness of the world, and whose substance is that of an idol, which waxeth old and shall perish in Babylon, even Babylon the great, which shall fall" (D&C 1:16). Brigham Young gave this counsel concerning material wealth: "The worst fear I have about this people is that they will get rich in this country, forget God and His people, wax fat, and kick themselves out of the Church and go to hell. This people will stand mobbing, robbing, poverty, and all manner of persecution and be true. But my greatest fear is that they cannot stand wealth" (Quoted in *The Miracle of Forgiveness*, p. 48).

PHYSICAL APPETITES AND PASSIONS

One of the greater gifts our Heavenly Father gives His children is a physical tabernacle. The corporeal bodies we receive as we slide through the veil to enter mortality have "built-in" drives and appetites. Learning to control them is one of the purposes of earth life. However, the veil largely hides this fundamental necessity. Here it is easy to believe that since a physical drive or appetite is inherent within these bodies of flesh and blood, therefore it should be fully expressed and explored. Some people today maintain that to restrain our carnal drives is unnatural or even psychologically damaging. The veil makes such arguments seem logical.

Satan's Goal

Besides our natural drives and appetites, our bodies are subject to Satan's enticements. He constantly uses his powers to exploit the physical appetites already found within our tabernacles. He knows it is possibly the easiest way to destroy the potential for a celestial resurrection which is the designed destiny of our mortal bodies.

We know that Satan and his followers are envious of our bodies. Satan will never receive a body and therefore his progress is stifled forever. Joseph Smith explained: "The devil has no body, and herein is his punishment. He is pleased when he can obtain the tabernacle of man, and when cast out by the Savior, he asked to go into the herd of swine, showing that he would prefer a swine's body to having none" (*Teachings of the Prophet Joseph Smith,* p. 181).

Undoubtedly, Satan rejoices if he can entice any of us to abuse our bodies and spoil the purpose for which they were made. His approach to them might be likened to a couple of young boys. The first receives a brand new bicycle for his birthday. The second boy is jealous since he has no bicycle. He tells the first that it is a lot of fun to ride around the new building being constructed. He knows the pleasure will be short-lived because there are many nails and broken pieces of glass and metal there which will certainly damage his tires. The first boy takes the bike to the construction sight and has fun riding around until he notices the tires are going flat. He is forced to walk the bike home and leave it in the garage because it is entirely incapable of fulfilling the purpose for which it was built. The second boy has gained nothing, but his jealousies are pacified as the two youngsters subsequently romp together with comparative equality. From then on the first boy is forced to play without the benefits which were once within his grasp and the jealousies of his (so-called) friend are subdued.

Uncontrolled Appetites

Built in to our physical bodies are certain drives assuring procreation. The Lord has specified their usage: "Wherefore, it is lawful that [a man] should have one wife, and they twain shall be one flesh, and all this that the earth might answer the end of its creation; And that it might be filled with the measure of man, according to his creation before the world was made" (D&C 49:16-17). Abuse of this power is rampant around us. Carnality is the result as people abuse their bodies through promiscuity, homosexuality, and sexual experimentation of every kind.

The veil hides the fact that the perceived pleasure provided by sexual deviations is extremely short-lived. The Lord has plainly taught that the only beings who will enjoy "eternal increase" or the ability to create spirit children after the resurrection are those who strictly observe the law of chastity and are sealed by proper authority in one of God's holy temples (see D&C 131:1-4, 132:19-20). The resurrection will completely remove procreative powers from all the spirits raised to the Telestial, Terrestrial or lower Celestial Glories. We are taught that gender is eternal, but for those resurrected to these lower kingdoms, the practical differences between the sexes may be far less significant than what we are accustomed to here on earth. President Joseph Fielding Smith explained: "Some of the functions in the celestial body will not appear in the terrestrial body, neither in the telestial body, and the power of procreation will be removed. I take it that men and women will, in these kingdoms, be just what the so-called Christian world expects us all to be—neither man nor woman, merely immortal beings having received the resurrection" (*Doctrines of Salvation*, 2:28).

Within our society we can identify individuals who plainly demonstrate what happens when physical appetites completely dominate the spirit. Paul rightly observed that there are some: "Whose God is their belly" (Philippians 3:19). It reminds me of a story that happened to a friend of mine named John. Shortly after receiving his driver's license, John was asked by one of his buddies to pick up his car from the local shop. The car was a souped-up Chevy with a 426 cc race-car engine. When John arrived to get the car, he discovered that it was parked next to the repair shop at the end of an alleyway which opened into a busy street. John had to back the car up the entire length of the alley because there wasn't sufficient space to turn it around. He got the keys and started the engine. He'd never driven such a powerful vehicle before. After putting it into reverse, he gently let out on the clutch. Before he knew it, the car had zoomed completely through the alley and had crossed one lane of traffic to land high-centered across the median in the road. Luckily there were no cars in the front of the alley or there would have been a collision. However, John then found himself blocking both lanes of traffic. Only with some assistance from the shop owner was he able to extricate the car from the median. It was clear to him that he had been unprepared for the incredible power the car possessed.

Today, though it occurs unconsciously, it seems that some spirits are equally overwhelmed by the powers within their physical bodies just as my friend was overtaken by the power of the Chevy he was asked to drive. Such people become consumed with the sensations a mortal body can generate, allowing those feelings to control their spirits, without realizing what is really happening. Their every thought and pursuit may be focused upon the carnal. They seem like five-year olds trying to drive an Indy 500 race car, incapable of coping with the power and capabilities of the vehicle. Perhaps such individuals will be consigned to drive something like a skate board through eternity because they will have demonstrated, during mortality, that they are unable to control anything grander. We might also imagine the turmoil they will experience in the Spirit World and beyond as their carnal addictions persist after their mortal bodies are taken from them.

Besides sexual perversions, other physical abuses are common on earth. Here some humans treat their bodies like a child would a new toy. In many ways the analogy holds true because we lived for millions of years as spirits in the premortal world. In contrast, we receive a physical body for a relatively short 70 years or so. As a consequence, many of these tabernacled spirits want to push every button and pull every lever just to see how it feels or to experience what will happen. Some take illicit drugs, while others get hooked on tobacco or alcohol. The veil has caused us to forget that these physical bodies are gifts from God. They are temples of the Holy Ghost (1 Cor. 6:19).

If Satan is unsuccessful in destroying our bodies' eternal potential, he may settle for a second approach. Since the veil conceals the fact that we should be shaping our bodies for Celestial glory, we may be tempted to focus all our energies enhancing their Telestial beauty and ignore the future.

The adversary may entice us to worship our bodies directly, to "worship and serve the creature more than the Creator," (Romans 1:25) thereby distracting us from the work we were sent here to do. It is good to maintain our bodies—to keep them attractive and healthy. But if these goals displace eternal priorities or cause us to worship our bodies directly, we will experience immense disappointment when the veil is lifted.

SATAN'S POWER IS TEMPORARY

Currently Satan and his followers entice us, looking in at us in our veil-lined cells. They can see us, but we can't see them. This arrangement is, of course, temporary. Someday we will know them for who and what they are. Then we will all resent them. But for some, it will be too late.

The Lord has promised: "The day soon cometh that ye shall see me, and know that I am; for the veil of darkness shall soon be rent, and *he that is not purified shall not abide the day*" (D&C 38:8; italics added). In that day it will take little effort to renounce *materialism* as fire melts the earth and everything upon it. Then it will be easy to repudiate *egotism* as every knee bows and every tongue confesses that Jesus is the Christ (see Mosiah 27:31). Subsequently, it will be easy for men and women to control *physical appetites* as they see their mortal tabernacles moldering in the grave or later as they rise in the resurrection with brand spanking new Terrestrial or Telestial bodies.

6

The Veil of the Heart

We have examined the veil of eternity which conceals external realities from our consciousness. This is not the only veil which constantly affects us. Other veils exist. These veils are largely inside of us, though they are intimately associated with the external veils we have discussed. They are also very important.

In the Book of Mormon we read of King Benjamin. He presided at a very important conference of the Church. He gave an inspiring discourse which is found in Mosiah 2-5. His words had a profound effect upon his listeners:

> And now, it came to pass that when King Benjamin had thus spoken to his people, he sent among them, desiring to know of his people if they believed the words which he had spoken unto them.
>
> And they all cried with one voice, saying: Yea, we believe all the words which thou hast spoken unto us; and also, we know of their surety and truth, because of the Spirit of the Lord Omnipotent, which has wrought a mighty change in us, or in our hearts, that *we have no*

more disposition to do evil, but to do good continually
(Mosiah 5:1-2; italics added).

On this occasion, the Nephites received a great blessing. They lost the "disposition to do evil," and acquired the desire "to do good continually." As each of us struggles daily with our sins, it may be hard to imagine such a state. To truly lose the "disposition to do evil" would transform most of us into the persons we are constantly striving to be. To have this blessing occur instantly during mortality would be a great benefit. What might we do to obtain it?

The account above tells us that the process which transformed the Nephites caused their *hearts* to change. If that is all that is required, we might ask: "Why don't we just change them? Why don't we flip off the top of our hearts to evaluate their contents and then go about purifying all we find there?" The answer is a *veil*. A veil firmly conceals the contents of our hearts from our minds. Furthermore, it prevents any direct manipulation of things found within. Yet if our hearts are the key to perfecting ourselves, to losing "the disposition to do evil," then perhaps this veil is the most important of all the veils.

THE VEILED HEART

The scriptures often speak of the *heart*. It appears to be a distinct entity from the minds of men and women. We think with our minds, but it is within the heart that our innermost nature is found. The two are inseparably divided by a barrier or veil:

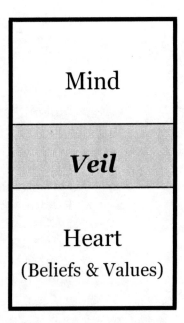

Though it is veiled from our minds, the heart is not a complete mystery. There is much we can learn about it.

Qualities of the *Heart*

The *heart* reflects specific qualities which powerfully affect the individual who possesses them.

The Righteous Heart:	Scriptural References:
Pure	Psalms 24:4, Matt. 5:8
Clean	Psa. 51:10, Prov. 20:9
United	Psalms 86:11
Broken	Psalms 51:17, 2 Ne. 2:7
Softened	D&C 121:3-4
Lowly	Alma 37:34, Moro. 7:43
Meek	Alma 37:33-34
Rejoicing	Psa. 119:111, Jer. 15:16
Sincere	Moroni 10:4
Courageous	Alma 62:1
Holy	Mosi. 18:12, D&C 46:7
Swollen	Alma 17:29, 19:13
Joyful	Job 29:13, Ecc. 5:20
Thankful	D&C 62:7
Honest	D&C 8:1, 11:10
Glad	Psalms 16:9, D&C 59:15
Opened	D&C 64:22
Right	Acts 8:21, D&C 40:1
Upright	Psalms 7:10, D&C 61:16
Cheerful	Ecc. 11:9, D&C 112:4
Comforted	2 Thes. 2:17
One	Jer. 32:39, Ezek. 11:19

The scriptures also describe the *heart* as evil and disobedient as shown in the following scriptures:

The Evil Heart:	**Scriptural References:**
Lustful	Proverbs 6:25
Firm	Job 41:24
Double	Psalms 12:2
Wicked	Deut. 15:9, Prov. 6:18
Proud	Prov. 21:4, D&C 42:40
Stony	Ezekiel 11:19, 36: 26
Blind	Eph. 4:18, D&C 58:15
Stout	Isaiah 10:12
Stubborn	Alma 32:16
Devil-lead	Alma 39:11
Uncircumcised	Acts 7:51, 2 Nephi 9:33
Unbelieving	D&C 58:15
Doubtful	D&C 58:29
Murmuring	D&C 75:7
Vain	D&C 106:7
Angry	1 Nephi 16:38
Puffed up	2 Nephi 28:9
Deceitful	Jeremiah 14:14
Unsteady	Helaman 12:1
Corrupt	D&C 10:21
Troubled	D&C 98:18
Hardened	1 Nephi 16:22, 17:30

Each of us may ask : "What qualities does my own heart contain?" We might easily identify a few, but we could not give a complete accurate inventory. Neither can we remodel or revise the inclinations located there. The veil directly impedes our efforts.

Core Beliefs and Values

From the foregoing lists, we can see that our hearts contain important personal qualities. Specifically the scriptures speak of the heart as the receptacle of our innermost *desires* (Alma 41:3, D&C 137:9 Mosiah 18:10-11), our private *intents* (D&C 6:16, Alma 18:32, D&C 33:1) and our intimate *affections* (Alma 37:35-36). Stated more simply, our hearts contain our core *beliefs* and *values*.

For years psychologists have taught that our minds are divided into both the conscious portion where we think and reason and an "unconscious" part which contains memories, thoughts, beliefs and values. The "unconscious" is completely hidden from the "conscious" section by a barrier. Carl Jung, a prominent psychologist explained: "[A] part of the *unconscious* consists of a multitude of temporarily obscured thoughts, impressions, and images that, in spite of being lost, continue to influence our conscious minds" (*Man and His Symbols*, p. 18; italics added).

Conscious
Barrier
Unconscious (Beliefs and Values)

Psychology's Model of the Mind

There appears to be a parallel between the conscious/unconscious model and the scriptural descriptions of the *heart* and *mind*.

Regardless, something exists within us which contains our innermost beliefs and values. It is hidden from our conscious thoughts by a barrier or veil. It may be referred to as the "unconscious" or as the *heart*. One of the primary purposes of mortality is to pierce this veil, to learn what our *hearts* desire, and to purify them.

Conscious		**Mind**
Barrier	Compare	*Veil*
Unconscious *(Location of core beliefs and values)*		**Heart** *(Location of core beliefs and values)*

THE INFLUENCE OF THE VEILED HEART

Earlier we discussed how things located outside the veil of eternity continually affect us. Our hearts (and all they contain) also constantly influence our decisions. Every day we make hundreds of choices. Many of them require our conscious deliberation, but most of them seem to occur almost "automatically." Because they seem automatic, we may forget they are, in fact, choices we must make. To illustrate, consider the following scenario:

I am building a dog house. As I pound in a nail, I strike my thumb. The pain is great and I curse loudly.

In the split second occurring immediately after smashing my finger, many responses were available to me. As my thumb throbbed with pain, I could have calmly exclaimed, "Mercy, how vexing." I might have said nothing at all or silently counted to ten. I could have jumped up and down, pulled funny faces or even danced a "jig." A great variety of reactions were available to me, yet, I chose to swear and yell.

The question arises, "In that brief moment, why did I choose to curse instead of reacting more appropriately?" For me, I must first admit that despite the pain, I never lost my free agency. It was my choice, my decision to swear and shout. I am the only person controlling my mouth and the words that come out of it. At no time did I relinquish control of my mouth to some external force.

Nevertheless, in that instant it is unlikely that I felt "in control" because there was no time for my conscious mind to deliberate upon the different reactions available. So we ask, "What was 'in control' if it was not my conscious mind?" The answer is found deep inside me. In that split-second, my thoughts, speech and body seemed to be under the complete control of another internal part of me. It was my veiled *heart*. When I smashed my finger and profaned, my behavior was essentially under the control of the beliefs and values found there. Dozens of reactions were available to me, but my heart determined which I would respond with. In this manner, the contents (or "programming") of our hearts are instantly and constantly manifested in all our "quick decisions."

It is apparent that in the episode above, the pain inflicted by the hammer was sufficient to exceed the pre-set threshold for swearing found within my heart. In that fraction of a second, the *value* (veiled from my mind) of the violent response was greater than the *value* (also veiled) of the spiritual and emotional peace which was automatically lost by the outburst.

This example is not uncommon among the Latter-day Saints. I know several active members who will swear only if a situation reaches the appropriate level of frustration or difficulty, then watch out. Otherwise, they refrain. Of course there are many others who never encounter a situation which causes them to value a response laced with profanity. The difference is found within their hearts.

Additional Examples

Consider the following examples of situations where there isn't time for our minds to reflect upon a decision that must be made. These examples demonstrate additional instances where the beliefs and values of our hearts are plainly manifest within our lives.

Jane gets pulled over by a policeman for going 40 miles an hour in a 30 mile-per-hour zone. The officer asks her if she knows the speed limit. She does.

Quick decision: Does she (1) say she doesn't know the real speed limit to avoid getting a ticket or (2) tell the truth and make herself look even more guilty for speeding?

Bob is talking with his in-laws who suggest in veiled tones that he is a poor provider for their daughter.

Quick decision: Does he (1) immediately become offended and leave the room or (2) exercise restraint and patience and try to refocus the topic of conversation?

Jerry is tired and arrives home from a long day at work. The house is a mess.

Quick decision: Does he (1) bluntly ask his wife, "What have you been doing all day?" or (2) with a smile and a hug inquire "What can I do to help?"

Karen watches the clerk at the market ring up her purchases one by one. The charges are plainly displayed on the register. All of a sudden Karen notices that one of the prices entered is lower than it should be.

Quick decision: Does she (1) say nothing since the store prices are too high anyway or (2) immediately point out the discrepancy?

Kent is walking alone through snow and ice. He trips and violently hits the pavement. The fall has torn a large hole in his suit trousers while lacerating his knee and scraping his hands.

Quick decision: Does he (1) get up angry, venting his frustration with vocal profanities or (2) quietly rise with silent disappointment?

Jennifer and her twelve-year-old daughter are at the movies. Her daughter is short for her age and the ticket seller charges her the admission price for an eleven-year-old.

Quick decision: Does she (1) quickly correct the mistake which would cost her a couple of dollars more or (2) ignore the discrepancy thinking short people should be charged the same as children anyway?

John is driving to work. A car cuts in front of him.

Quick decision: Does he (1) honk the horn and tailgate the car until it turns or (2) realize the driver needs some extra room and back off?

Sherry's sixteen-year-old son is horsing around the kitchen table when he accidentally spills a glass of juice.

Quick decision: Does she (1) criticize him and demand that he immediately clean up the mess or (2) realize it was unintentional and quietly toss him a towel to wipe it up?

Daniel is swimming with some friends. A pretty girl in a skimpy bathing suit walks by.

Quick decision: Does he (1) turn for a prolonged double-take or (2) remain undistracted (maybe sing a hymn)?

Salley is a homemaker with four children. She discovers her five-year-old has just written all over a piece of new furniture with an indelible marker.

Quick decision: Does she (1) yell at the child and spank him or (2) control her temper while administering consequences?

Larry just finished giving his Gospel Doctrine lesson at Church. Afterwards, several members of the class come up to thank him for what they have learned, praising his efforts.

Quick decision: Does he (1) beam with pride and explain how glad he is that members appreciate the hours of preparation he has made, or does he (2) express thanks (knowing the Holy Spirit is actually responsible for any enlightenment obtained) and humbly change the subject?

"Quick Decisions" are Heart Reflexes

These are just a few examples which demonstrate how many of the quick decisions we make daily are in fact "reflexes" controlled by the beliefs and values veiled within our *hearts*. Everyone is conscious of the fact that we are born with specific *physical* reflexes. Undoubtedly we are aware that if a person hits the tendon just below the knee cap, his lower leg will "jerk" forward. In physically healthy people, "reflexes" such as these are constant and undeviating. They are a result of a "reflex arc" which is a series of nerves within our bodies which complete a specific circuit. As long as this circuit is undisturbed, a particular stimulus (e.g., tapping the knee) will initiate electrical impulses which will travel the predetermined route to specific muscles always resulting in the same response (e.g., a knee jerk).

In a similar manner, each of us possesses our own set of reflexes which influence the things we say and do. They virtually guarantee that we will respond to a specific set of circumstances in a distinctive way. These responses occur without any prior deliberation and in this they seem almost "automatic." They are not governed by unchangeable nerve tracts within our bodies but are mediated by our *hearts*. Therefore, we might think of them as "*heart* reflexes."

"*Heart* reflexes" differ from our physical reflexes in two respects. First, physical reflexes are neither good nor bad, while "*heart* reflexes" can be either. Second, our physical reflexes are literally beyond our control. No matter how hard we try, we cannot prevent the reflex, such as a knee jerk, from occurring. "*Heart* reflexes," however, change as the contents of our hearts are changed.

The Global Influence of the Heart

A second manner in which our *hearts* influence our lives is seen globally in our prevailing goals and priorities. Besides our quick decisions, the contents of our hearts will always be visible within our lives in more general ways. That is to say that the unconscious beliefs and values of the heart will always find their way into our thoughts, speech and actions. They determine the basic direction our lives are taking. They are responsible for our sensitivity (or the lack thereof) to spiritual things. They also affect our moods and feelings.

A plain example of this power of the *heart* was demonstrated to me several years ago. A friend of mine and I were members of the same Elders Quorum. The quorum president had challenged the members to review the upcoming lesson in the priesthood manual prior to the next quorum meeting. One evening during the subsequent week, my friend recalled the challenge but really didn't feel like reviewing the lesson. Instead, he preferred to watch an interesting sports event on television. As he remembered the quorum president's challenge, he encountered some guilt about the preferences he felt inside. As he thought about his situation, he realized that he *wanted to want* to study the lesson manual, but what he really *wanted* to do was to watch sports on TV. The inner conflict ended with him watching sports. Later, as he shared the story with me, I could detect that he continued to feel some guilt about his decision, but it seemed overshadowed by the frustration he felt over his inability to change his innermost desires. So often we find that changing our hearts involves changing what we *want* for what we *want to want* (or ought to want).

My friend experienced the power of his *heart*. That night he discovered his core value was to watch sports. That value was found within his heart and was, under those circumstances, stronger than the value to study the gospel. Even though his mind acknowledged the disparity, his heart prevailed. This story illustrates the significance of the heart and one way its contents will always be manifest in our lives.

The Heart is Powerful

The Lord taught: "For where your treasure is, there will your heart be also" (Matt. 6:21). The things we value within our hearts represent our "treasure." Elder Oaks has commented: "Not only will the righteous desires of our hearts be granted, but also the unrighteous desires of our hearts. Over the long run, our most deeply held desires will govern our choices, one by one and day by day, until our lives finally add up to what we have really wanted" (*Pure in Heart*, p. 51).

The Savior explained: "A good man out of the good treasure of his heart bringeth forth that which is good; and an evil man out of the evil treasure of his heart bringeth forth that which is evil: for of the abundance of the heart his mouth speaketh" (Luke 6:45). "For with the heart man believeth unto righteousness" (Romans 10:10). But if a person's heart is evil, wickedness will grow out of it as well: "For out of the heart proceed evil thoughts, murders, adulteries, fornications, thefts, false witness, blasphemies" (Matt. 15:19). (See also Mark 7:21, 12:34.)

A wise person once warned: "Beware of what you really want, for you shall have it." What we "really want" is reflected by the beliefs and values found within the veiled heart. Even though our hearts are veiled, their influence is not. Their contents will be plainly manifest in our lives in some form or another.

The Heart Is Veiled

Within the scriptures, and other inspired writings, we often encounter helpful warnings about the importance and influence of the heart. It seems a little ironic, however, to note that little is said about the veil which conceals it from our minds.

If the heart is the key to our righteousness, then it seems the veil hiding the heart is also important. It is the barricade we must penetrate. Piercing this veil permits us to understand our hearts and thereby comprehend ourselves, and to purify our innermost desires, beliefs and values.

Ignoring the Heart

Any person attempting to discover what lies in his own heart will quickly find out exactly how thick and dense the veil covering it is. He will also quickly realize that the heart, even if uncovered, is very complicated. These two characteristics make it very easy to ignore. Consequently, many people simply refuse to believe that there are any unconscious forces (arising from our hearts) working within them. They may go through life pushed and pulled by unseen influences, which emanate from their own hearts, without realizing what is going on.

Such individuals may still accomplish much including incremental improvements. Positive changes always involve the heart but can occur without our being aware of it. Nevertheless, by denying the reality of the heart, they also deny themselves the ability to go to the actual root of the problems they see in themselves.

7

An Introduction to the Heart

We may be surprised to learn about the existence of the heart. To realize that there is something hidden inside each of us which exerts great power over us may be astonishing. Nevertheless, it is true. We may call it the *heart* or use the term "unconscious." Regardless, it is veiled from our minds, yet is very real and very important.

So we seek an introduction to our own hearts. If we could somehow dissolve the veil and peer within, what would we find? Not only could we identify specific contents, but we might also view how our hearts actually function. This chapter will attempt to give a brief overview of the veiled heart.

OUR BELIEFS AND VALUES

In the last chapter we observed that our hearts are filled with our innermost "beliefs and values." More specifically, all kinds of traditions, ideas, teachings, desires and standards have permeated through the veil of our hearts to currently dwell within them. We may wonder where they came from. The beliefs and values we currently hold within our hearts obviously arrived there sometime in the past. It appears that some of them originated with us in the premortal world while others have been acquired during mortality.

Premortal Beliefs and Values

At birth our hearts were not barren receptacles waiting to receive whatever mortal influence might descend upon them. We developed beliefs and values during our premortal existence. When our spirits left the premortal realms traversing the veil (of eternity) to dwell within a physical tabernacle, many of our premortal beliefs and values accompanied them into mortality to reside within our hearts.

We recall that President Benson taught: "We bring from our premortal state various talents and abilities" (*Teachings of Ezra Taft Benson*, p. 484). President Heber J. Grant also explained: "The labors that we performed in the [premortal] sphere that we left before we came here have had a certain effect upon our lives here, and to a certain extent they govern and control the lives that we lead here" (*Teachings of Latter-day Prophets*, p. 496). President Joseph Fielding Smith observed: "Environment and many other causes have great influence on the progress and destiny of man, but we must not lose sight of the fact that the characteristics of the spirit which were developed through many ages of a former existence play a very important part in our progression through mortal life" (ibid, p. 496).

Good and Evil Beliefs and Values

The beliefs and values found within the heart can influence our lives in one of three ways, (1) for good, (2) for evil, or (3) in neutral ways. *Neutral* beliefs are of themselves neither good nor bad. Such beliefs and values often reflect our own personal biases like our favorite color, food or season of the year. They bring variety into our lives as they allow us to be different without compromising righteousness.

False beliefs and wicked values enter our hearts through the enticings of Satan. Moroni expounded: "But whatsoever thing persuadeth men to do evil, and believe not in Christ, and deny Him, and serve not God, then ye may know with a perfect knowledge it is of the devil; for after this manner doth the devil work, for he persuadeth no man to do good, no, not one; neither do his angels" (Moroni 7:17). False beliefs and evil values will always result in sinful thoughts and behaviors.

All *true* beliefs and eternal values come from our Heavenly Father. They have existed throughout eternity and will exist eternally. Through the Holy Spirit they are constantly available to us, to our minds and hearts.

Influences of Mortality

During mortality we are constantly bombarded with notions and ideas from nearly innumerable sources within our environment. Almost unconsciously, the *traditions* held by those in our family or by close friends permeate into our hearts. Traditions by themselves are neither good nor bad. But they can easily promote evil or good to flourish within the hearts of a society or civilization. Paul encouraged the Thessalonians to "hold the traditions which ye have been taught" (2 Thes. 2:15). But traditions can easily lead us into iniquity: "And that wicked one cometh and taketh away light and truth, through disobedience, from the children of men, and because of the tradition of their fathers" (D&C 93:39; see also Mosiah 1:5, D&C 74:4).

Other sources of influence are seen throughout our environment. We may obtain beliefs and values from friends, teachers, and most anyone we come in contact with. Cultural norms and the standards of the civilization where we are raised will sway our hearts.

The most important influence upon our beliefs during mortality should be the Holy Spirit. It represents the greatest force on this planet to change our beliefs so they reflect truth and reality. Impressions from the Holy Spirit are perceived as He communicates directly to our spirits which dwell within our mortal tabernacles.

Reactions—An Important Source of Beliefs and Values

Many, perhaps most, of the beliefs and values found within the heart were not adopted uncensored. That is, we seldom hear an idea and immediately embrace it intact. Most of what we espouse within our hearts is filtered by our hearts before it is embraced. In this way, our hearts function as their own security guards and content censors. Accordingly, our *reactions* to our surroundings are the actual source of our heart's contents rather than the surrounding influences themselves.

CONFLICTING BELIEFS AND VALUES

Besides the direct influence of the beliefs and values of our hearts, they interact with each other, often creating conflicts. Conscious conflicts occur when we find ourselves torn between two values, like wanting to attend Church but also wishing to watch a football game on TV at the same time. But a multitude of conflicts may exist beyond our consciousness in the deep recesses of our hearts. Though they are unseen, they are not unfelt.

Inner Conflicts Between Good and Evil

One obvious conflict occurs when we value contradictory things, like good and evil. The clash between good and evil is the *basic* conflict here on earth. Such conflicts destroy inner peace and produce guilt. This should not surprise us because God has designed it to be so. He has given us our consciences which create an inner conflict any time we contemplate evil. "For behold, the Spirit of Christ is given to every man, that he may know good from evil" (Moroni 7:16). This is a blessing for those who wish to keep the commandments.

However, we have our agency. We may choose to not only disregard the influence of our consciences, but we can push the conflicts they produce out of our minds. That is, we may shove them beyond the inner veil to reside in the concealed portions of our hearts. Consequently, they may seem to be hidden and therefore less bothersome to us.

Consider the husband who values (#1) his marriage, but also values (#2) dominating his wife or being excessively critical. Or the wife who values (#1) her marriage, but values (#2) retaliation for any of the multitude of inconsiderate things he may do to her as well. Then there is the teenager who values (#1) morality and spirituality, but also values (#2) his friends and their activities which may lead to unrighteousness. We must choose, and even after a choice is made, the conflict may still rage in our hearts. Regardless of what we choose, good or evil, if we subsequently continue to value the opposite ideal, we will not be at peace with ourselves. Consequently, conflicts are often very emotionally taxing.

Marriage Creates Conflicting Family Values

Many seeds of future inner conflict are acquired during our childhoods. Interacting in the family setting powerfully affects our hearts, infusing them with family values. However, our parents and families are not perfect. Traditions, standards and coping mechanisms we adopt as children may actually prove to be counterproductive to us as adults. Since they are instilled within our hearts, we may not realize their true nature. They may continue to influence us into our adult years, but will not help us grow and progress as we otherwise might.

A common clash of these inbred family values occurs in marriage. We may say: "My family did it this way." But what we are thinking is: "My family did it this way so it is the only *right* way." It may or may not be right, but it seems right because of its predominant position within our hearts. Marriage automatically creates these kinds of conflicts. How we deal with these differing standards reflects our maturity. It also determines our ability to enjoy a deep and satisfying relationship with our spouses.

Defenses Against Low Self-esteem Create Conflicts

People with low self-esteem may encounter many inner conflicts within their veiled hearts. Defending themselves from their feelings of inferiority may create desires and actions which conflict with other general goals. It seems most of us suffer from lower levels of self-esteem. Hence, these conflicts are very common.

One defense mechanism commonly adopted involves portraying an image to those around us. I may be unhappy with my real self and consequently attempt to project an image of a person who is better than I actually am. For example, a woman in the ward may strive to be "Supermom" or "Suzy-homemaker." The image she strives to portray requires her to arise before anyone else, maintain impeccable make-up and grooming, keep an immaculate house, bake (wheat) bread, do canning, sew her own clothes and those of her family, do her visiting teaching, be frugal, visit the sick, care for the aged, attend the temple, do her genealogy, raise perfect children, search the scriptures, and be an effective Relief Society President all at the same time. Over time her self-image may be completely engulfed by the image she has adopted. At that point, maintaining it might become her primary endeavor in life. Successfully projecting the image becomes paramount.

A problem will eventually (years to decades) arise though because she is not the same person as her image. The image is a mirage. It is unreal and conflicts invariably occur when reality collides with unreality. These collisions constantly develop but most of them occur beyond our consciousness. The veil consistently shields us from genuine inner rivalry occurring within the expanse of our hearts.

Eventually, the real self becomes submerged beneath layer after layer of pretense. Nevertheless, it is not easily destroyed. The belief and values of the real self will continually conflict with the beliefs and values of the image, almost indefinitely.

The conflicts resulting from living an image may be concealed by the veil, yet we deeply feel their effects. Life loses its meaning despite the many sacrifices and accomplishments we lay at the feet of the image. Chronic tension and anxiety might be felt. A profound feeling of emptiness and futility may follow. Our physical and emotional energy might be consumed. Discouragement, despair, numbness and depression may result without us realizing why.

Church Callings Provide Images

In the Church, every calling we receive carries an image we may choose (consciously or unconsciously) to maintain. We can all envision the image of a good home teacher or a good visiting teacher. We may also imagine a dutiful bishop, Sunday school teacher, Primary president, or choir director. Individuals who strive diligently to uphold the image will often accomplish much good.

However, several problems will usually appear. First, it is possible that upholding the image will conflict with the inspiration of the Holy Spirit. The Spirit could inspire us in a direction which is inconsistent with the image we wish to project. Images like to be in the spot-light, a location the Spirit will seldom guide us to. Second, the issue of sincerity emerges. A friend of mine once jokingly advised: "Be sincere even if you don't mean it." Such a motto might apply to anyone striving to uphold an image of righteous service. Service is rendered, but primarily to maintain the image, not from genuine charity. An important third consideration involves the almost inevitable result of serving an image. Serving any false god brings little real growth or progress. The individual easily becomes "burned out" or disillusioned, not only with the calling, but sometimes with the Church itself.

Promoting an image makes us do the right things for the wrong reasons. Instead we should seek pure motives which arise from a pure heart. Charity is the key, but developing it is not spontaneous. Perhaps this is why Moroni admonished us that we might "pray unto the Father with all the energy of heart, that ye may be filled with this love" (Moroni 7:48).

Inner Conflicts are Ubiquitous

Almost everyone possesses conflicting values within their hearts. James warned: "A double-minded man is unstable in all his ways" (James 1:8). Perhaps these constant underlying conflicts are a major source of emotional chaos in our world today. As they smolder and fester within us, they zap our emotional strength and weaken our resolve to righteous action. Satan is no doubt aware of this truth. He knows it is an effective way to make us miserable and hinder our progress.

Another blessing of a "pure heart" is not just eliminating false beliefs and wicked values, but in possessing beliefs and values which are congruent with one another. This is a key to overcoming inner conflicts. We must find out who we are—children of our Heavenly Father—and then pursue righteous personal priorities.

OTHER IMPORTANT CONTENTS OF THE HEART

To gain a more complete picture of the heart and its contents, we must address four additional feelings which may be stored there. Specifically they include: *fears, anger, guilt* and *unexpressed suffering.* These are different from many of the beliefs and values we have referred to because they are usually concealed within our hearts for a specific purpose: emotional survival.

For reasons which are sometimes difficult to discern, we may banish specific feelings into hidden inner realms of the heart where we are no longer required to consciously deal with them. Some psychologists refer to this as "stuffing it."

When this occurs, the inner veil becomes a form of insulation between them and our conscious thoughts. However, it is a porous partition. Even though they may exist out of mind, they are not extinct. They may constantly exert an immense negative influence over us.

Unconscious Fears

Exaggerated *fears* are very common. The Lord realized that they can exist within our hearts, easily preventing us from progressing as we would like (see D&C 67:3).

Naturally, we should fear things which might harm us spiritually or physically. However, during our formative years we might embrace fears of things which are not inherently fearful. We may fear things, people, places, or circumstances which should not normally cause fear. Psychologists call extreme forms of them "phobias." They can greatly limit a person's behavior and progress. More subtle fears can also be found in our hearts.

Brigham Young counseled: "You need have no fear but the fear to offend God" (*Discourses of Brigham Young*, p. 71). Yet how easily fear may enter our hearts. Fears of poverty, of rejection, of the unknown, of embarrassment or humiliation are very common. Our needless fears may secret themselves in some obscure corner of our hearts, only to dash out at a moment's notice, directing our feelings and thoughts in useless or harmful paths.

Repressed Anger

Unexpressed *anger* is often encountered. We are taught to avoid anger: "[W]hosoever is angry with his brother, shall be in danger of his judgment" (JST Matthew 5:24). And we are commanded to love: "Thou shalt love thy neighbor as thyself" (D&C 59:6).

Nevertheless, we are not perfect. Most of us do get angry sometimes. When we feel anger, it is usually wise to acknowledge it and attempt to dissipate it in the best way possible. Yet, such a course requires us to admit to ourselves that we are indeed angry which is tantamount to admitting we are not following the admonitions of the Savior. This is a difficult admission.

In contrast, some individuals will choose a second course. It consists of simply denying the anger and stuffing it somewhere behind the veil of the heart. This action permits them to preserve a facade of righteousness and eliminates the need to confront their undesirable feelings. However, relegating our anger to a hidden position within our hearts is invariably problematic. Repressed anger is very toxic and will usually manifest itself eventually. Its later expression can easily be more harmful than if it had been acknowledged and expressed in an acceptable manner when initially felt.

Guilt

Another common harmful belief involves guilt. Guilt is profitable if it incites us to repent (2 Cor. 7:10). But rather than repent, we may choose to push the guilt behind the veil where it is less noticeable.

Besides constructive guilt, other forms of guilt may be found within the heart. How often do we believe we are guilty when we have committed no offense? Or how easily do we retain guilt for transgressions we have truly repented of? It is so natural sometimes to withhold forgiveness from ourselves, even if we effortlessly forgive others.

Our feelings of inappropriate guilt (whether conscious or unconscious) may prevent us from fully embracing the atonement of Christ within our lives. We may simply believe we are unworthy of it. Psychologists refer to a process of "self-hate" which may greatly impede emotional maturing and inner peace.

Unsuffered Suffering

The heart veil can also conceal a great deal of unsuffered suffering. Commonly we encounter traumatic situations as children which are difficult to bear emotionally. The death of a loved one, family turmoil including divorce, abuses (especially sexual abuse) and other problems may simply overwhelm a child's ability to cope. In order to survive emotionally, the youth may need to sequester the pain away. But as we have observed, it does not evaporate.

The presence of unsuffered suffering in the heart can easily create a generalized numbness. By deadening ourselves to the pain, we may deaden all our emotions. However, if we are to find peace and joy, we will usually need to face the pain. The Lord can help us; sometimes professional counseling is needed.

THE HEART IS COMPLEX

This brief introduction to several different aspects of the veiled heart quickly reveals that it is very complex. Understanding it can be as challenging as comprehending advanced statistics, neurosurgery, corporate law or perhaps nuclear physics. Even for individuals bent on understanding and improving their own hearts, the challenge is enormous.

The Heart is Very Complicated

Several reasons help explain why the heart is so complicated. First, the sheer number of distinct beliefs, thoughts, feelings and ideas it contains may be immense. Second, the contents of our hearts are constantly expanding. The process of living involves new experiences which provide new beliefs and values to form within us. Third, the beliefs and values come in all sorts of sizes, shapes and colors. That is, a large variety also exists. The spectrum includes things which are true and things which are false and everything in between. Fourth, the individual contents of the heart may interact with each other in complicated ways. Fifth, some things may be hidden in our hearts that our minds really don't want to know about. Usually we have bonafide reasons for isolating them from our conscious thoughts. However, while quarantined, they are not lost or inactive.

Perhaps the greatest deterrent to understanding our own hearts stems directly from the veil. On top of all the complexities listed above, the veil requires us to garner clues about our hearts like Sherlock Holmes solves a murder mystery. We begin our investigation not only lacking answers, but often also lacking the right questions.

Why Understand the Heart?

In light of these difficulties, many people may have little desire to understand their own hearts. Grappling with the inner veil to understand and change what lies within it may seem too exhausting. This being the case, we might ask, "Why should I seek to understand my own heart?" The answer stems from the great power it wields in our lives.

The Heart—the Key to Purity and Inner Peace

We have already reviewed the great influence of the heart in our thoughts and actions. Truthfully, to study our hearts is tantamount to studying everything that makes us who and what we are. The heart is preeminent in our individual quests to triumph over self. Specifically, it is the key to increased purity and inner peace.

Any progress we make to perfect ourselves involves the heart. Any man (or woman) who genuinely seeks perfection will eventually come face to face with his concealed heart. This paradox, produced by the veil, occurs as our conscious desires conflict with our heart-controlled flesh. We may desperately wish to escape our sinful thoughts and behavior, but struggle to generate sufficient righteous thrust to escape the gravity of our impure hearts. We may feel to lament as Nephi: "O wretched man that I am! Yea, my heart sorroweth because of my flesh; my soul grieveth because of mine iniquities. I am encompassed about, because of the temptations and the sins which do so easily beset me" (2 Nephi 4:17-18).

Besides righteousness, our hearts are also the key to inner peace. Any additional endowment of inner peace we may receive comes as our hearts are changed. This endowment is realized as inner conflicts are resolved and harmful emotions dispelled.

Hence, anyone who wishes more holiness and/or inner tranquility will have to deal with his own heart. He may not realize what is happening, but his heart will be at the heart of any success.

Delving into a study of the human heart is daunting. Happily, we need not approach it alone. "God is greater than our heart, and knoweth all things" (1 John 3:20). He has promised: "And if men come unto me I will show unto them their weakness" (Ether 12:27). These weaknesses are found within our hearts. Equally, the Lord has assured us that He will assist as we strive to improve our hearts: "A new heart also will I give you, and a new spirit will I put within you: and I will take away the stony heart out of your flesh" (Ezekiel 36:26).

Challenges From Both Sides of the Veil

So far we have learned how feelings hidden by the *veil of our hearts* can create conscious challenges. We have also observed how Satan and his imps prowl outside the *veil of eternity* enticing us to misery and sin. We do most of our living between these two veils. Truly we might seem to live "between a rock and a hard place" here in mortality.

8

Veils and Our "Private Worlds"

It may seem that the veil of *eternity* and the veil of our *hearts* are basically unrelated to each other. Perhaps some will suppose that their only similarity is that they might each be called a "veil." However, the two veils are closely related. First, it appears that many Saints will experience the destruction of both veils at about the same moment in the future. Second, both veils are necessary in order to make mortality a probationary state. Third, our minds, with all their thoughts, understanding and knowledge lie on one side of both veils. On the other side of the veil of eternity we find an "outer reality." On the other side of the veil of our hearts is an "inner reality." Our minds are tucked neatly in between. Besides these similarities, the two veils also interact with each other in an interesting way.

CHOOSING OUR OWN REALITIES

Because the veil hides eternity and the eternal reality from each of us, we cannot readily take our bearings from eternity as we sojourn here on earth. Locked inside this outer veil, we must each decide precisely what we will believe concerning the things hidden beyond it. We cannot escape this burden which is placed upon us. Individually, we must each determine what we believe is out there. This we have done whether we realize it or not. Each one of us has already decided what we believe concerning God, and things before and after mortality. The beliefs we hold are stored within us and influence everything we think, say and do.

Some people may disagree, saying they have never considered such questions. Nevertheless, it is impossible to remain undecided or uncommitted regarding these things. Even indecision is a decision, because indecision can govern our lives as easily as any of the other choices we make.

The Veil as a Canvas

When I was in high school, I helped with the school musical. Several scenes required different painted backdrops to be made. The canvases had to be exceptionally large in order to cover the entire rear portion of the stage. None of the canvases were all that thick, but they successfully concealed everything behind them. When lowered, it was impossible to determine what additional props or participants were hidden at the back of the stage. Neither could the rear doors or the back wall be identified. But whenever the backdrops were lifted, we saw what really existed back there.

Besides hiding everything behind them, the canvases served another even more important purpose. The artwork upon each one had the power to create a whole new world upon the stage. A great deal of work was required to complete them. When finished, each depicted a different scene. One was outdoors of a palace. Another was of an inner chamber. When lowered, they transformed the stage into a different realm. Everyone knew it wasn't the real world, but its effects were successful enough to temporarily convince the audience.

In some ways, the veil hiding eternity is like these canvases (before they were painted). Our five senses cannot detect what lies beyond it, neither can we tear it away. Consequently, we must decide what to believe concerning all that it conceals. Our personal responses to the questions: "Where did I come from?" "Why am I here?" "Where am I going when I die?" "Is there a personalized God?" "Is Satan real?" reflect our innermost beliefs. As such, they are strokes of paint against the canvas veil of eternity. Together they form the scenery, even a sort of landscape, for our own "private worlds." This is where we actually live—in our own "private worlds."

To escape our private worlds and join the "real world" would require us to destroy the veil of eternity. Since this is impossible, we are forced to create our own worlds. This occurs as we embrace beliefs about eternity.

The veil also hides eternal values. We cannot easily detect things which are eternally useful. Hence, we must choose what we think is valuable. It is easy to do within the shadow of the veil, within our private worlds.

The beliefs and values which pervade our private worlds are stored (you guessed it) within our veiled hearts.

Our Hearts Project Our Private Worlds

An experience I had as a child might provide another analogy. I remember trying an experiment with my brother. It was a dark, overcast evening and our family and relatives had just finished watching some old 8 mm films. When they were done, we transported the movie projector out the front door using an extension cord. Subsequently we shined the beam of light up in the air and tried to focus the image on the clouds above. We figured the cloud-screen would be a few hundred feet wide. Unfortunately, the bulb was not very bright so the light rays just disappeared into the darkness. Yet, had we been successful, we might have approximated the effect of our hearts as they interact with the veil of eternity. Our hearts are the projector and the film is comprised of our innermost beliefs and values. Figuratively, they are projected upon the screen of the veil (of eternity) which encloses us. Hence, we do not detect the eternal reality, instead our hearts project our personal realities.

Our hearts also create the atmosphere within our private worlds. In the same way, they control the lighting, the coloring, the shadows, the viewing perspective and everything else which determines our perception. Our innermost beliefs and values constantly bias our views and slant our vision. Therefore, we seldom perceive the furnishings, the people or any of the props within our private world truthfully. This helps explain why there are so many different opinions about things, so many different feelings, so many different ideas.

Every private world is different from every other because every heart (and its contents) is different from every other. There are literally millions of variations regarding the beliefs and values we may embrace through mortal time.

Private Worlds—"Level the Playing Field"

Paul taught that Heavenly Father sends each of us to earth having "determined the times before appointed, and the bounds of [our] habitation" (Acts 17:26). We know that the Father is just, but we may wonder how mortality can be fair when some people are born into such prosperous conditions and others are forced to spend almost every waking moment simply providing for their basic physical needs. So many distinct variables exist within the individual environments where we are born: language, skin color, food, climate, traditions, religious beliefs, access to truth, etc. We may ask: "How can mortality be equitable with so many differences?"

Our premortal accomplishments explain a great deal of the disparities found in mortality. However, life is a probationary state for all of us. "[T]here was a space granted unto man in which he might repent; therefore this life became a probationary state; a time to prepare to meet God; a time to prepare for that endless state which has been spoken of by us, which is after the resurrection of the dead" (Alma 12:24). Our environment is important, but the battles we fight with evil, with *materialism, egotism* or *physical appetites*, occur in the privacy of our private worlds.

In many ways, the composition of our private worlds will

determine the eternal world we inherit after we are resurrected, whether it be Telestial, Terrestrial or Celestial. The
scriptures suggest that even while living on earth, we are
already complying with the laws of one of these three kingdoms and are being "quickened by a portion of the glory" of
them (D&C 88: 29-32). Possibly the constant renovation of
our private worlds relates to our perfecting work, that we
may "establish [our] hearts unblameable in holiness before
God, even our Father" (1 Thes. 3:13).

Perhaps the veil serves to "level the playing field," in
some measure, by demanding that we individually decide
what to believe and live accordingly, no matter our physical
surroundings.

THE VEIL OF ETERNITY—
THICK OR THIN

Our innermost beliefs regarding eternity may or may
not correctly identify what lies beyond the veil. When we
embrace false beliefs (lies), we thicken the veil and separate
us further from eternal truth. Our private worlds become
darker as the Light of Christ dims within us. "For they love
darkness rather than light, and their deeds are evil, and
they receive their wages of whom they list to obey" (D&C
29:45). Concerning the wicked, Brigham Young explained:
"[I]gnorance covers them as with a mantle, shuts out the
light of truth from them, and keeps them in darkness; and
if the light were to shine upon them, as it does now and as
it did in the days of the Apostles, would they receive it? No,
they would not. Light has come into the world, but the
wicked choose darkness rather than light. Why? It was told
in days of old that their deeds were evil. That is the fact

today—'They choose darkness rather than light, because their deeds are evil,' and their hearts are fully set in them to do evil" (*Discourses of Brigham Young*, p. 79).

Examples of false beliefs, which enhance darkness, include atheism or theories based upon organic evolution. Such teachings deny the premortal and postmortal realms as well as the existence of God and the devil. Accordingly, they paint the veil with the darkest pitch.

For some, darkness provides an illusion of security, like the thief who waits for the dead of night to obscure his wicked activities. Perhaps he feels like an ostrich concealing its head in the deep dark soil, believing he is completely hidden from everything in the light. But the darkness is temporary, awaiting the Second Coming of the Light of the World.

Embracing Truth—Thinning the Veil

In contrast, when we use faith to embrace eternal truth, we are not simply painting the veil, but actually *excavating*. The veil thins before us so truth from eternity can enter into our private worlds. The dissolving veil allows the light of eternity to burst forth to illuminate our own personal reality until the eternal reality completely overtakes it and they become one. The Lord explained:

That which is of God is light; and he that receiveth light, and continueth in God, receiveth more light; and that light groweth brighter and brighter until the perfect day (D&C 50:24).

And if your eye be single to my glory, your whole bodies shall be filled with light, and there shall be no darkness in you; and that body which is filled with light comprehendeth all things (D&C 88:67).

He that keepeth his commandments receiveth truth and light, until he is glorified in truth and knoweth all things (D&C 93:28).

COLLIDING REALITIES— INTERACTING WITH OTHERS

Understanding the fact that we live within our own private worlds is helpful when dealing with others. If the veil prevents me from embracing the eternal reality, it also prevents other people from doing so. Consequently, we are all suffering from near-sightedness, not experiencing the real world, but living in the private worlds we have created.

Understanding Other People

A knowledge of private worlds helps us comprehend why people behave the way they do, especially when what they do seems so strange to us. In short, *people do what they do for a reason* and the reason is found within their private worlds, within the beliefs and values they have accumulated within their hearts. If their actions seem bizarre to us, then we must crawl into their worlds and experience their realities. We may find some darkness there, but it is probable that there will also be light which can illuminate our own private worlds in some way. Only by perceiving their worlds can we accurately interpret or even critique their behavior.

Gaining access to other people's realities requires that

they let us into their hearts. They will need to trust us. So we must listen and observe without judgment. Much time is generally needed. If our spouses, children or co-workers dumbfound us, then we haven't taken the time to understand their worlds, because the things they do make sense to them and are apparently appropriate within the realities they experience.

Through many prolonged sincere efforts, friends and loved ones may eventually give us a peek into their private worlds. Upon crossing the threshold, we must be careful not to touch the furnishings or criticize the decor. We are all very sensitive to critiques of our private worlds. For us, they are temples; they are sacred ground. At some future date, after we have shown sustained respect for their quarters, they might let us handle their belongings and maybe even help them renovate or clean up.

Most of us fiercely defend our personal realities. They represent our own truth and reality no matter what is going on outside of them. Some people seem to spend their entire lives trying to validate their private worlds. They may go to great lengths to prove to themselves and to others that they have already embraced truth. But too often they are just fooling themselves.

Changing Other People's Private Worlds

For a person to change, he (or she) must change the private world he lives in. This of course requires a change of heart. There is no other way. However, it is common for us to try to directly change others, to instantly bring their private worlds in line with our own. When people do things that "bug" us or that we otherwise do not approve of, we may attempt to reach out and quickly eliminate that behavior. However, trying to change another person's world without his trust or permission is like trying to clean or renovate a house by standing in the front yard. We might successfully reach through a window to straighten a few items on a table, but the owner will soon return and replace those items to the positions where his heart has already determined they should go. Hence, the journey to help another change does not begin with a list of things for them to do, since we can hardly make recommendations regarding a house we have never visited. We begin only as we commit the time required to gain their trust and confidence.

Sometimes we may fool ourselves into thinking that we have a special ability, maybe x-ray vision, which allows us to sense what modifications another person should make. But without having visited his private world, we will be making mostly useless suggestions. He may thank us, but he will leave us believing that our recommendations are for someone else because they just don't seem to fit his private world. Usually he is right.

These principles help us to understand why people change so slowly. We know how hard it is to change ourselves, the immense effort and time required to penetrate our hearts. Changing others requires even more of our resources because we must first be invited into their private worlds. From there, we might more accurately understand what they hold in their hearts, remembering that our own beliefs and values will bias our judgments. We must possess their trust and only then will they be open to suggestions.

Conflicting Worlds

Understanding the reality of private worlds explains how there are few conflicts between people, but many conflicts between peoples' worlds. This realization spawns patience and tolerance. When confrontations arise, we can more easily identify the magnitude of the obstacles involved. Or if we are trying to help someone improve himself, we should understand the scope of the job we have assumed. Usually it is an immense task. It might be useful to approach it like a foreman who is asked to move a mountain. He is not frustrated that it can't be done in one day. That would be totally unrealistic. However, he knows that the mountain can be moved if the proper equipment and adequate time is allowed, that is, truck load by truck load (or "line upon line").

Too often we may feel that if another person would quickly adopt our view, a disagreement would be solved. But changing his view may require modifications, sometimes great modifications in his private world which require a change of heart. Such changes do not happen quickly. Knowing this, patience and tolerance become logical responses and impatience and intolerance appear pointless.

Some pious individuals may believe they are justified in forcing their beliefs and values upon someone else because they already have embraced so many truths. They may feel they live more in the eternal world than in their own private one. This feeling might seem to justify coercing others to be like us (because we are so wonderful!). Notwithstanding, as a person embraces more and more eternal truth so that his or her personal reality approaches the eternal reality, an immense respect for *free agency* will emerge. Manipulation, coercion and compulsion will be seen as useless and disgusting (maybe even Satanic; see Moses 4:1, 3). That person will become a light to others, not a judge of their private worlds. He will understand the duration of *long* in long-suffering. Meekness and submissiveness will be his friends.

9

Truth and the Heart

Understanding that the heart is the key to perfecting ourselves helps us realize the importance of penetrating the veil which covers it. The veil of the heart is naturally very thick. It constantly prevents us from accomplishing two important tasks. First, we cannot instantly evaluate the contents of our own hearts. That is, we cannot take an accurate inventory of all contained there. It is impossible to identify the lies (false beliefs) and the undesirable values we have in our hearts. Neither can we readily tabulate those which are useful and desirable, those which cause us to behave admirably.

The second thing the veil of the heart prevents is direct manipulation of the contents of the heart. Even if we could identify what was in there, the veil would still prevent us from throwing out undesirable and conflicting values and false beliefs. We could not cut out an especially poisonous value like a surgeon so effectively excises a gangrenous gallbladder or an infected appendix. Nor could we subsequently drive down to the neighborhood HEART STORE to purchase new values and beliefs to replace the old ones. Even identifying and scrutinizing the good beliefs and values we desire does little to catapult them through the veil into our hearts.

What if we found an ancient bottle lying in the sand in a remote part of the Middle East? What if we rubbed the bottle and a Genie appeared to grant us two wishes? If our first wish was to request that the veil of the heart be instantly removed, what would we find? How would our lives be changed if for our second wish, we were given full power to change our heart's contents directly any way we wanted? We have no Genie, but these two wishes can become realized through the Holy Spirit and our own intense efforts.

THE BELIEFS AND VALUES WE SEEK

As we seek to improve the beliefs and values within our hearts, it is helpful to understand more precisely what we want to have within them. Obviously, we don't want any false beliefs (lies) or evil values. Our goal is to infuse true beliefs (or eternal truth) and eternally useful values. A heart possessing these things is called pure and holy.

Eternal Truth

We might inquire, "What is truth?" and "Where do we find it?" The question: "What is truth?" was posed to the Savior by Pilate shortly before the crucifixion (John 18:38). The Savior apparently did not respond to his question, but philosophers have speculated and haggled about the answer for centuries.

In reality many different "truths" exist today but not all are eternally useful. Consequently, just because something may be labeled "truth" does not mean that it deserves space in our hearts. For example, "historical truth" flows from the work of researchers who examine records and journals from the past. Likewise, "scientific truths" are determined from experiments and investigations, from observation and inquiry. Such "truths" may or may not be helpful to us, to our hearts.

The Doctrine and Covenants identifies the "truths" we are looking for: "And truth is knowledge of things as they are, and as they were, and as they are to come" (D&C 93:24). That is, truth is knowing the past, present and future as they really exist within their own respective time frames. For example, if we ask, "What exactly constitutes 'things as they were'?" we would conclude the past "reality" is discovered by recalling not only the past millennia since the earth was created, but also the premortal realm which is now hidden by the veil. Likewise, understanding "things as they are" would necessitate the acknowledgment of things now veiled from our minds, of God and His angels in addition to Satan and his followers. The scriptures tell us they are "in our midst" (D&C 38:7) and "round about" (D&C 76:29) us here on earth. Comprehending "things as they are to come" would require a view of the Spirit World, the resurrection, and beyond. The veil of eternity keeps the knowledge of these truths from our minds.

Here again we discover a way in which the two veils interact. In chapter three we discussed faith and how it involves "reaching" through the veil to grasp truths now found in eternity. However, for our faith to grow, both veils are actually involved. First the veil separating us from eternity must be pierced, thus exposing our minds to new eternal truths. Second, we must allow those truths to penetrate into our hearts which, in effect, involves a second veil (the one between the mind and the heart).

The Focus of Eternal Truth

If all the truth we seek originates in eternity, what might happen if the veil of eternity was instantly removed, thus allowing us to somehow detect the truth we cannot now discern? Without the Holy Spirit we could not understand very much of what would be presented to us. But if a person could understand all the truth found in our premortal past, our current sphere and the future, he or she would instantly grasp two important concepts: (1) the complete design of the Plan of Salvation and (2) our absolute need to comply with its requirements. This is truth. It is eternal. It is what we seek.

When grasped within our hearts, eternal truth automatically directs our thoughts, speech and actions so they comply with the Plan of Salvation. Truth dissolves undesirable "heart reflexes" and also influences our hearts "globally," pointing us towards perfection during mortality and Celestial glory eternally. These are the goals of the Plan of Salvation.

Truth Can Be Believed Forever

Eternal truth is valuable because it will never change. Truth is truth no matter on which side of the veil it is found. The Lord observed: "All truth is independent in that sphere in which God has placed it" (D&C 93:30). Therefore, truth is not changed in time (mortality) or eternity. That which is true can be believed in the premortal world, embraced during earth life (within our hearts) and possessed on into the Spirit World and beyond the resurrection without compromise or alteration.

This knowledge helps us to realize that any belief which is not true will have to be discarded at some point in the future. Joseph Smith stated it quite plainly: "To become a joint heir of the heirship of the Son, one must put away all his false traditions" (*Teachings of the Prophet Joseph Smith*, p. 21). We might speculate how we will eventually cast off all our untrue beliefs. But we can be certain that no falsehoods exist in the Celestial Kingdom. The Prophet also taught: "Every principle proceeding from God is eternal and any principle which is not eternal is of the devil" (ibid p. 181). Hence, another definition of truth might be: "Anything we can embrace, believe and enjoy during mortality and for all eternity.

The Veil Hides "Truth"

JESUS CHRIST: "I AM...THE TRUTH"

Another "truth" exists. The Holy Writ contains the Savior's declaration concerning the relationship between Himself and truth: "Jesus saith unto him, I am the way, the truth, and the life" (John 14:6). We might inquire as to how Jesus is "the Truth."

Christ qualifies as "the Truth" in several ways. First, as the Redeemer of all mankind, He put the Father's plan, "the Plan of Salvation," into effect. We can see how the Plan of Salvation is truth because it incorporates the premortal world, progresses through mortality and proceeds through the Spirit World to the resurrection and describes things on both sides of the veil. It plainly reflects "things as they are, and as they were, and as they are to come" (D&C 93:24). Through His atonement and resurrection Christ made this "truth" (the Plan of Salvation) operative throughout all the eternities. Through His sacrifice it becomes "truth" and He is an integral part of it. (See Heb. 12:2.)

Christ—The Perfect Example

Jesus Christ is truth in another important way. To understand how, we must remember that from the very moment of His spiritual creation as the "Firstborn" of our Heavenly Father, He has set the example for us. As premortal spirits living for ages and eons in that realm, we all deviated from the laws given to us there. Yet even as we faltered, Christ remained in full compliance with all the Father's commandments. He lived as an example of truth and of Heavenly Father's plan. Nevertheless, He was a spirit and our Elder Brother. Even before we were born into mortality, Christ was there showing us the way.

Christ was born upon this earth as the Father's "Only Begotten Son." His heart was pure from the beginning—no false beliefs, no wicked values, no conflicting desires or useless fears invaded His heart. Here, He advanced "from grace to grace, until he received a fulness" from Heavenly Father (D&C 93:12-14). That "fulness" undoubtedly included eternal truth which flooded His heart.

With His pure heart, the Savior was perfect in keeping the commandments during mortality. He also received every ordinance, including baptism and those given in the temple. Joseph Smith observed: "If a man gets a fullness of the priesthood of God he has to get it in the same way that Jesus Christ obtained it, and that was by keeping all the commandments and obeying all the ordinances of the house of the Lord" (*Teachings of the Prophet Joseph Smith*, p. 308).

Regardless of the moment we choose to examine, whether in the premortal eternity or during His earth life or beyond, Christ was (and is) in complete compliance with all the requirements of the Father's plan. At no time has He varied in the slightest from our Heavenly Father's highest expectations. Jesus told the Nephites: "I have suffered the will of the Father in all things from the beginning" (3 Ne. 11:11). By following Christ's example in time and eternity, He shows us "the Way" and represents "the Truth" for all God's spirit children. He was and is a manifestation of that truth, a personification of that truth.

Embracing Truth—Emulating Christ

Accordingly, embracing true beliefs within our hearts will lead us to be like Christ, to directly fulfill His admonition: "Therefore, what manner of men ought ye to be? Verily I say unto you, even as I am" (3 Ne. 27: 27). Any teaching, idea, dogma, philosophy, theory, doctrine or conviction which encourages us to be like Christ, is centered in eternal truth and is worthy of our hearts. Yet some of these teachings will not mention Christ by name.

They may seem entirely secular, but if they entice their adherents to become as Christ is, they are based upon truth.

Specifically, we find truth in any teaching which extols being:

humble	kind
charitable	patient
diligent	gentle
easy to be entreated	merciful
long-suffering	full of love
submissive	chaste
honest	virtuous
benevolent	lovely
meek	temperate

No matter the process, anything which encourages us to genuinely reflect these qualities is teaching us eternal truth and bringing us to Christ. President Joseph F. Smith believed that we were foreordained to embrace all of these characteristics so that we too could be as Christ is:

Christ is the great example for all mankind, and I believe that mankind were as much foreordained to become like Him, as that He was foreordained to be the Redeemer of man... It is very plain that mankind is very far from being like Christ, as the world is today, only in form of person. In this we are like Him, or in the form of His person, as He is the express image of His Father's person. We are therefore in the form of God, physically, and may become like Him spiritually, and like Him in the possession of knowledge, intelligence, wisdom and power (*Gospel Doctrine*, p. 18; see also Romans 8:29).

Paul instructed that God has: "chosen us in Him [Christ] before the foundation of the world, that we should be holy and without blame before Him in love" (Ephesians 1:4).

Observing that the Plan of Salvation teaches us of the need to be like Christ, we can distill the preceding discussion down into one sentence: "Eternal truth invariably (1) prompts us to be like Christ or (2) it convinces us of the need to be like Christ." Hence, embracing truth in our hearts invariably purifies them, purifying us and making us pure as Christ is pure (1 John 3:2-3).

DISCOVERING THE CONTENTS OF OUR HEARTS

We know we want eternal truth and eternally useful values within our hearts. We also know we don't currently possess them all. The process of eliminating undesirable components within our hearts and replacing them with worthwhile ones is called "purification." Purifying our hearts starts as we earnestly attempt to discover the impurities found within. Then, as we identify the truths that need to replace them, we work to embrace them. Three sources exist which can help us discover the contents of our hearts.

Our Consciences

Many of the undesirable contents of our hearts are already known to us. Our consciences tell us about them. This is an important part of God's plan. "For behold, the Spirit of Christ is given to every man, that he may know good from evil," Mormon taught (Moroni 7:16). Most of us can easily write a rather lengthy list of our faults and weaknesses. These occur because our hearts are not pure. Such a list represents an important starting point for purification.

Listening To Others

Another useful source of information comes from other people. They see us differently than we see ourselves. They often know about the many "blind spots" we possess concerning our own speech or behavior. It is possible that they can help us remove the rosy-colored glasses we may use to critique our own strengths and weaknesses.

The apostle Paul instructed the saints in his day: "Them that sin rebuke before all, that others also may fear" (1 Timothy 5:20). We don't hear too much "rebuking" in the Church these days, despite the fact that we all are imperfect. Receiving counsel from others requires a lot of humility. Even when offered sincerely with the intent to help us progress, it is easy to take offense. By so doing, we may miss a great opportunity for self improvement.

Some people may benefit from assistance from professional therapists and counselors. The focus of psychologists is often to make unconscious things conscious. In other words, to expose the contents of our hearts to our minds so we might deal with them directly.

Approaching God

The most important source for learning about our hearts comes from our loving Heavenly Father. He has promised: "And if men come unto me I will show unto them their weakness. I give unto men weakness that they may be humble; and my grace is sufficient for all men that humble themselves before me; for if they humble themselves before me, and have faith in me, then will I make weak things become strong unto them" (Ether 12:27). Before we can have "weak things become strong," we must have those weaknesses "shown" to us. This the Lord has assured us He would do.

Questions such as, "What am I doing right now which is most offensive to my Heavenly Father?" will be answered as we ponder, pray, read the scriptures and involve the temple in our lives. President Harold B. Lee has counseled: "The most important of all the commandments in the gospel to you and to me is that particular commandment which for this moment requires in each of us the greatest soul searching to obey. Each of us must analyze his needs and begin today to overcome, for only as we overcome are we granted a place in our Father's kingdom" (*Stand Ye In Holy Places*, pp. 215—216).

So we strive to discern unwanted values and false beliefs. We embark upon the journey by discovering our greatest weakness. Then "line upon line, precept upon precept" (2 Ne. 28:30), we continue the quest to distinguish all that hides there.

10

Changing the Heart

Changing our hearts requires us to change the beliefs and values found within them. We wish to reach through the veil to substitute truth for false beliefs and eternal values for carnal ones. The battlefield is within us, but the success or failure is manifest in our behavior and our thoughts. Our efforts may proceed from the outside-in with *discipline* or from the inside-out by *changing perspective*.

USING *DISCIPLINE*

The most common approach to changing our hearts involves directly replacing more desirable *behavior* for that which we currently display. Each time we are tempted with an unacceptable thought or action, we simply substitute a more acceptable one. Eventually the new behavior will permeate through the veil of our hearts to change the values hidden there.

Examples are everywhere. If I have a problem with

swearing, I can force myself to not profane. Perhaps my wife will demand a dollar every time I curse, giving me added motivation. We know that our hearts are changed when the more desirable behavior comes automatically. At that point we conclude that we no longer *value* swearing within our hearts. This approach can be applied to almost any obvious weakness.

Discipline is the Key

The key to success in substituting is *discipline*. Discipline describes all the internal strength, will-power, self-control, personal restraint, dedication, persistence, determination, fortitude, intensity and stamina which we may recruit to effect an outward change. It includes everything we can muster to force external conformity with a new standard. We use discipline to change undesirable thoughts, speech and action.

Discipline brings our behavior into compliance like sandbags direct an errant river, guiding the forceful current down a path to the predetermined destination. But in this example, discipline also supplies the sandbags, the work of hauling the sand, shoveling it into the bags and then lugging them to their sites. With sufficient discipline, our behavior can be channeled on a route leading to genuine change. Discipline empowers the person to intercept the continual influence of the undesirable beliefs and values found within the heart. Eventually even our hearts are changed.

Utilizing discipline to suddenly change an old pattern of behavior or thought is not easy. Old habits and routines are usually firmly rooted within the values of our hearts.

Therefore, to make the initial "substitutions," where an old behavior pattern is instantly replaced with new, will require significant effort until the heart is finally transformed.

Steps To Follow

Several steps may help us as we use discipline to infuse new values into our hearts:

1. Identify the old imperfect behavior to be changed.
2. Identify the new desired behavior to substitute—be very specific.
3. Set a goal to replace the new for the old—ask for divine assistance.
4. One-by-one when occasions arise to follow the old standard, consciously substitute the new behavior (remember discipline).
5. Persist until the new standard permeates the veil of the heart to change the values found there (remember discipline).

Popular and Easy To Begin

This approach to changing our hearts is very prevalent. Its popularity stems from the ease with which it may be started. The first three steps outlined above can be commenced in a split-second. A person needs only to identify a particular flaw and then set a goal to abolish it. It is that simple. As a process, it requires virtually no forethought. We may uncover a personal defect and then almost instantaneously tell ourselves we should stop. Then the process has begun.

Of course, simply setting a goal does not assure that the goal will be attained. The last two steps in this approach require incredible amounts of discipline or little change will ultimately result.

Each of us is capable of generating discipline in sufficient quantities to change our hearts. But our own personal wells of discipline do not spring eternal. Therefore, we must learn how to best apply the discipline we possess to the changes we wish to accomplish. Like any other "tool," using discipline effectively requires practice and experience. The Lord's counsel: "Do not run faster or labor more than you have strength and means" (D&C 10:4; see also Mosiah 4:27) applies. So does the observation that changes usually occur "line upon line; here a little, and there a little" (Isaiah 28:13) within our lives.

Satan Is Very Persistent

Sometimes in our quest to overcome our sins, we may be fooled concerning our previous effectiveness. We may believe our hearts have been transformed, but then discover in the moment of temptation that our efforts had not permeated into them. This occurs because Satan is far more patient than we are and knows the extent of time required for discipline alone to change our hearts. He has also learned that our dedication and self-control may deteriorate before our hearts are truly transformed. Patiently, he may await the hour when our guard is lowered, then seizing the opportunity, he may successfully tempt us. Then the need for additional persistence will be plainly evident.

God Requires Discipline

Despite the obvious limitations associated with the use of discipline to change the heart, it is required by our Heavenly Father. Just because it may be difficult and strenuous, if not inefficient, we cannot dispense with it while waiting for other methods to change our hearts. "If you keep not my commandments, the love of the Father shall not continue with you, therefore you shall walk in darkness" (D&C 95:12). "For I the Lord cannot look upon sin with the least degree of allowance" (D&C 1:31). It is an eternal, universal law.

CHANGING THE HEART
BY CHANGING PERSPECTIVE

Another approach to changing our hearts involves changing our perspectives. If we could view our weaknesses and imperfections with an *eternal perspective*, they would instantly appear differently to us. This is what we try to do.

By obtaining an eternal perspective of our weaknesses, we come to understand how they fit in the "big picture." To see them in the light of eternity causes them to appear undesirable, illogical, useless and counter-productive. Why? Because all the consequences and eternal compromises they bring are also dragged into our view. Our sins stand before us naked in all their ugliness.

Such a viewpoint reveals sin to be an enemy of everything with eternal worth. It divests sin of its veneer of fancy apparel and worldly adornments. There exposed, sin is seen as it really exists, fleeting, inferior and spiritually destructive. Sinful endeavors are revealed in their true colors as futile, useless and even worthless. In contrast to righteousness, sin is identified as nothing more than a detour or a distraction. With such a perspective, sin becomes repulsive, disgusting, revolting and offensive and the truth about sin is known.

A clear view of eternity would permit us to easily weigh our sins on a scale of eternal value. Then we would easily understand that the perceived benefits are extremely temporary and could never justify the lasting destruction they invariably bring. Sin's impact throughout all eternity would be obvious. We would literally come to "shake at the appearance of sin" (2 Ne. 4:31). Engaging in sin would be similar to emptying a trillion dollar bank account for a one minute roller-coaster ride...it just isn't worth it. Who could believe it had value?

The Savior observed, "And ye shall know the truth, and the truth shall make you free" (John 8:32). One manner in which the truth can make us free comes as it liberates us from the belief that sin is desirable. Eternal truth, as revealed through an eternal perspective, also convinces us of the accuracy of Alma's observation that regardless of the sphere in which it is located, whether in time or in eternity, "wickedness never was happiness" (Alma 41:10).

Seeking God's Perspective

The new perspective we seek is simply God's perspective. He referred to His perspective: "Thus saith the Lord your God, even Jesus Christ, the Great I AM, Alpha and Omega, the beginning and the end, *the same which looked upon the wide expanse of eternity, and all the seraphic hosts of heaven, before the world was made*" (D&C 38:1; italics added). How would such a perspective change our views of iniquity and wickedness? This is what we seek, to view sin and all evil as God now does with an *eternal perspective.*

We often encourage our children, when they are confronted with temptation, to ask the question: "*What* would Jesus do?" Yet, it might be just as important to inquire "*Why* would He do it?" If we could embrace the "why," then the "what" would come automatically to us. The "why" is based upon an eternal perspective. We are reminded that this is the perspective of all future inhabitants of the Celestial Kingdom and they would undoubtedly benefit if they were to embrace it now.

God dwells in eternity, immersed in a realm which is perfused and saturated with truth (D&C 88:6, 12). The scriptures tell us that heaven is "on a globe like a sea of glass and fire, where all things... are manifest, past, present, and future, and are continually before the Lord" (D&C 130:7; see D&C 38:2). It is like a great Urim and Thummim (D&C 130:8). In such a realm, no sin could appear to be the least bit desirable. Even the "little sins" we presently keep back from the Lord would appear ugly and embarrassing. In that sphere, any deviation from purity would be seen as an intolerable aberration. This eternal perspective can be grasped during mortality.

Learning Is Required

To gain a new perspective requires that we learn new facts. Albert Einstein once said, "The significant problems we face cannot be solved with the same level of thinking we were at when we created them." Neither can we abandon our current weaknesses without abandoning our current "level of thinking" concerning them. Changing our "level of thinking" changes our perspectives of those weaknesses.

Acquiring the new perspective demands work. Seldom will a new perspective simply "pop" into our minds without any effort. Herein is the reasoning for the Lord's admonition to "study it out in your mind" (D&C 9:8) and to "study my word" (D&C 11:22). Through our efforts, new knowledge will come into our minds which can ultimately affect the things we believe and value, thus changing our perspectives and our hearts.

Heavenly Father Will Help

Our Heavenly Father will help us. We recall His promise: "And if men come unto me *I will show unto them their weakness.* I give unto men weakness that they may be humble; and my grace is sufficient for all men that humble themselves before me; for if they humble themselves before me, and have faith in me, then will I make weak things become strong unto them" (Ether 12:27; italics added). Is the Lord's offer to "show" us our "weakness" restricted to simply enlightening our minds concerning the contents of our hearts?

Perhaps. Nonetheless, it is possible that the Lord is also offering to *show* us our weaknesses in another way. He may be willing to *show* us our weakness in the light of eternity, letting us see how our imperfections fit in the eternal scheme of things. To receive a "wide-screen" cinema of our own sins would undoubtedly change our perception of them, enhancing our determination to annihilate them. The new beliefs and values we would grasp could then burn out the old ones which currently give rise to our sins and imperfections. Possibly this is one of the ways He will "make weak things become strong unto [us]."

The process for gaining additional understanding about our weaknesses involves the same activities as listed on pages 35-38.

LET GOD CHANGE OUR HEARTS

In chapter six we read about the Nephites whose hearts were instantly changed:..."the Spirit of the Lord Omnipotent... has wrought a mighty change in us, or in our hearts, that we have no more disposition to do evil, but to do good continually (Mosiah 5:1-2). It is natural for us to pray for such an event. If it could occur in our lives, it would be quick, easy and incredibly effective. Our hearts could be transformed and almost instantly we could become holy.

However, usually this is not the Lord's way. Changing our hearts is a process we are constantly engaged in. Purifying our hearts is called being "born again." For most of us, it will not be a single momentary experience. Elder Bruce R. McConkie observed: "We are born again when we die as pertaining to unrighteousness and when we live as pertaining to the things of the Spirit. *But that doesn't happen in an instant, suddenly. That also is a process. Being born again is a gradual thing*, except in a few isolated instances that are so miraculous they get written up in the scriptures. As far as the generality of the members of the Church are concerned, we are born again by degrees, and we are born again to added light and added knowledge and added desires for righteousness as we keep the commandments" (*Doctrines of the Restoration*, p. 53; italics added).

Therefore, men and women who seek perfection will find that their efforts to pierce the veil comprise a life-long task from which they cannot escape. Joseph Smith taught similarly that perfection "is a station to which no man ever arrived in a moment" (*Teachings of the Prophet Joseph*

Smith, p. 51). President Lorenzo Snow observed: "Latter-day Saints could not possibly come up to such a moral and spiritual standard [of perfection] except through supernatural aid and assistance. Neither do we expect that the Latter-day Saints, at once will, or can, conform to this law under all circumstances. It requires time; it requires much patience and discipline of the mind and heart in order to obey this commandment. And although we may fail at first in our attempts, yet this should not discourage the Latter-day Saints from endeavoring to exercise a determination to comply with the great requirement" (JD 20:188).

God's Assistance Is Real

Despite Heavenly Father's reluctance to single-handedly purify our hearts, He will assist us. As we individually strive to do it, we will feel His influence strengthening our discipline. We will also appreciate the whisperings of the Holy Spirit, teaching us and expanding our perspectives. At times, we may even believe He is indeed, reaching into our hearts to change them. His "eyes" and "ears" are upon us (1 Peter 3:12) and He truly does "care" for us (1 Peter 5:7).

EXPANDING TRUTH WITHIN
OUR HEARTS

We have learned that we can change our hearts through substitution, truth for lies, eternal values for false ones. We can also change our hearts in another way. It involves direct expansion. Our hearts are totally expandable. They can contain all the truth we can infuse into them. Just as the Savior's pure heart grew "from grace to grace, until he received a fulness" (D&C 93:13), so can each of ours. We qualify for God's "grace" as we strive to purify our hearts and our lives. Then we can embrace new truths within our minds and our hearts will expand to accommodate them. "For if you keep my commandments you shall receive of His fulness, and be glorified in me as I am in the Father; therefore, I say unto you, you shall receive grace for grace" (D&C 93:20).

The Lord has admonished us: "search the scriptures" (John 5:39). The promises are great:

> For thus saith the Lord: I, the Lord, am merciful and gracious unto those who fear me, and delight to honor those who serve me in righteousness and in truth unto the end.
>
> Great shall be their reward and eternal shall be their glory.
>
> And to them will I reveal all mysteries, yea, all the hidden mysteries of my kingdom from days of old, and for ages to come, will I make known unto them the good pleasure of my will concerning all things pertaining to my kingdom.
>
> Yea, even the wonders of eternity shall they know, and things to come will I show them, even the things of many

generations.

And their wisdom shall be great, and their understanding reach to heaven; and before them the wisdom of the wise shall perish, and the understanding of the prudent shall come to naught.

For by my Spirit will I enlighten them, and by my power will I make known unto them the secrets of my will yea, even those things which eye has not seen, nor ear heard, nor yet entered into the heart of man (D&C 76:5-10).

Our hearts can swell enough to contain "the wonders of eternity," even "all things pertaining to [God's] kingdom." But we must study and learn and *appeal* to the Holy Spirit (D&C 11:18).

When filled with such eternal truths, our lives will naturally become more holy. That holiness will permit even more and more truth to shower down through the veil of eternity, to pierce the veil of our hearts and change us eternally. "He that keepeth His commandments receiveth truth and light, until he is glorified in truth and knoweth all things" (D&C 93:28).

11

The Destruction of the Veil

No matter what we do during mortality, we cannot escape the effects of the veil. However, it is a temporary restraint.

LIFE WITHOUT THE VEIL

At some point in the future, the veil of eternity and the veil of the heart will be dissolved for every one of us. For the "just," it may well constitute the greatest moment of their entire existence (to that point). What great changes will be experienced then? First, premortal memories will be restored. Second, we will no longer view spiritual things as "through a glass, darkly" (1 Cor. 13:12). Viewing God the Father and His Son, as well as spirit entities like the devil and his followers will no longer be impeded. Third, our hearts will be purified, permitting us to become of one heart and one mind (D&C 29:13).

Regaining Our Premortal Memories

We have obviously forgotten the ages and eons we lived in the premortal realms, progressing and preparing for mortality and beyond. How wonderful it will be to regain the memories of our activities during that phase of our existence. Elder Neal A. Maxwell has written: "Among the 'all things [that] shall be restored' (Alma 40:23) will be memory, including eventually the memory of premortal events and conditions. What a flood of feeling and fact will come to us... [O]ne of the great blessings of immortality and eternal life will be the joy of our being connected again with the memories of both the first and the second estates (*Men and Women of Christ*, p. 132).

Our gratitude to Heavenly Father will increase. "When we get our premortal memories back," observed Elder Neal A. Maxwell, "these will give us further cause to be even more grateful to God—deepening in us the spirit of a perpetual Thanksgiving; for then we will acknowledge that God's justice and mercy have been perfect throughout the total span of our remarkable relationship with Him (see Mosiah 16:1; Alma 12:15). While for the moment we cannot recall our first estate, we can anticipate our third estate and its promised blessings" (*A Wonderful Flood of Light*, p. 57).

President Lorenzo Snow observed that part of the purpose of mortality is to "secure the position we occupied in the other life when we go back" (*Teachings of Lorenzo Snow*, p. 92). Hopefully, when our premortal memories are restored, we will discover that we have accomplished everything we aspired to while living in premortality.

Seeing Spiritual Realms

When the veil is lifted, we will then be capable of detecting spirit bodies just as we now can see physical bodies. This will allow us to view celestial beings, angels and unembodied spirits. Precisely how we will then relate to other eternal beings is difficult to imagine, but Joseph Smith taught: "that same sociality which exists among us here will exist among us there, only it will be coupled with eternal glory, which glory we do not now enjoy" (D&C 130:2).

Besides openly interacting with angels and righteous spirits, removing the veil will permit us to easily identify the devil and his followers and to know them for what they are. The righteous will have power over them (see D&C 29:29).

Removing the Veil of our Hearts

The veil covering our hearts will also be removed at some point in the future. Rather than speculate on the exact process, we might note that, for individuals already striving to keep the commandments, the ultimate result will be purification. Their hearts and minds will be pure, filled with truth and eternal values. Concerning the righteous on that day, the Lord has said: "[T]hey shall be purified, even as I am pure" (D&C 35:21).

This is necessary if we are to endure the Second Coming of the Savior: "But the day soon cometh that ye shall see me, and know that I am; for the veil of darkness shall soon be rent, and he that is not purified shall not abide the day" (D&C 38:8). The apostle John advised: "Beloved, now are we the sons of God, and it doth not yet appear what we shall be: but we know that, when He shall appear, we shall be like Him; for we shall see Him as He is. And every man that hath this hope in Him purifieth himself, even as He is pure" (1 John 3:2-3).

Possessing a pure heart will allow us to enjoy the blessing that Christ prayed for during the great intercessory prayer: "That they all may be one; as thou, Father, art in me, and I in thee, that they also may be one in us" (John 17:21; see also D&C 29:13, 35:2). This "oneness" is a great blessing. Brigham Young observed: "[T]he angels are of one heart and of one mind, in their faithfulness and obedience to the requirements of their Father and God. They can desire and ask for nothing that will make them happy, good and great that is withheld from them; and life eternal is theirs. Why, then, should they not be of one heart and of one mind? They see alike, understand alike, and know alike, and all things are before them, and, as far as their knowledge and experience extend, they see the propriety of all the works of God, and the harmony and beauty thereof" (*Discourses of Brigham Young*, pp. 41-42).

For the wicked, removing the veil of our hearts will be a "terrible" day (Joel 2:31). Enoch prophesied: "Behold, the Lord cometh with ten thousand of His saints. To execute judgment upon all, and *to convince all that are ungodly among them of all their ungodly deeds* which they have... committed" (Jude 1:14-15; italics added; see also D&C 99:5). "The rebellious shall be pierced with much sorrow" (D&C 1:3) and "tremble and shake to the center" (D&C 10:56). "[T]he nations of the earth shall mourn, and they that have laughed shall see their folly. And calamity shall cover the mocker, and the scorner shall be consumed; and they that have watched for iniquity shall be hewn down and cast into the fire" (D&C 45:49-50).

In addition, "the secret acts of men, and *the thoughts and intents of their hearts*" will be revealed for all to see, that is, if anyone really wants to (D&C 88:108-110; italics added). The contents of their hearts will condemn them. In contrast, John observed: "Beloved, if our heart condemn us not, then have we confidence toward God" (1 John 3:21).

Destroying Our "Private Worlds"

Earlier we noted that both veils seem to interact in such a way that each of us lives in a sort of "private world" during mortality. With the destruction of the veils, our private worlds will also be destroyed. For the righteous, it will be nothing more than the completion of the excavating efforts they were accomplishing during their mortal lives through discipline and faith. Light and truth will surround them. Then they will see things "as they really are" (Jacob 4:13) and they will be seen by others to be as they really are. No "private world" filters will distort their perspectives. Perhaps this is what the Lord meant when He said: "They who dwell in His presence are the Church of the Firstborn; and *they see as they are seen*, and *know as they are known*, having received of His fulness and of His grace" (D&C 76:94; italics added).

WHEN WILL THE VEIL BE REMOVED?

Considering the great and wonderful changes that await the righteous when the veils are removed, we may wonder when this will occur. Possibly, we might even look forward to the day.

Will the Veil Be Removed At Death?

On occasion, a Church member may believe that passing through the veil of death automatically eliminates all portions of the veil. Perhaps this idea is derived from Alma's statement that: "the spirits of all men, as soon as they are departed from this mortal body, yea, the spirits of all men, whether they be good or evil, are taken home to that God who gave them life" (Alma 40:11). If we are ushered back into God's presence, we would assume that the veil currently hiding His presence is permanently rent. President Joseph Fielding Smith explained: "These words of Alma as I understand them, do not intend to convey the thought that all spirits go back into the presence of God for an assignment to a place of peace or a place of punishment and before Him receive their individual sentence. 'Taken home to God,' simply means that their mortal existence has come to an end, and they have returned to the world of spirits, where they are assigned to a place according to their works with the just or with the unjust, there to await the resurrection" (*Answers to Gospel Questions*, 2:85).

Brigham Young suggested that as we burst through the veil of death, we *could* be privileged enough to see the Father and the Son. But that it was not automatic:

"I want to say to my friends, if you will live your religion, live so as to be full of the faith of God, that the light of eternity will shine upon you, you can see and understand these things for yourselves, that when you close your eyes upon mortality, you wake up right in the presence of the Father and the Son *if they are disposed to withdraw the veil*, they can do as they please with regard to this; but you are in the Spirit World and in a state of bliss and happiness... The spirits of the living that depart this life go into the world of spirits, and *if the Lord withdraws the veil*, it is much easier for us then to behold the face of our Father who is in heaven than when we are clothed upon with this mortality (JD 17:142-143; italics added).

For those who have not yet heard the gospel, a continuance of the veil is important. Their probations are not yet ended and the veil is requisite. "But blessed are they who are faithful and endure, whether in life or in death, for they shall inherit eternal life" (D&C 50:5). "For verily I say unto you, blessed is he that keepeth my commandments, whether in life or in death; and he that is faithful in tribulation, the reward of the same is greater in the kingdom of heaven" (D&C 58:2).

Elder Melvin J. Ballard instructed: "[M]en won't know any more when they are dead than when they are living, only they will have passed through the change called death. They will not understand the truths of the Gospel only by the same process as they understand and comprehend them here. So when they hear the Gospel preached in the Spirit World they will respond just as our fathers and mothers have, with a glad ear" (*Three Degrees of Glory*, p. 20).

Death will bring large changes, but it is probable that

most spirits of the dead will not be greatly enlightened, especially regarding the entire Plan of Salvation. It appears that for many, the remaining portions of the veil will remain securely intact.

Will the Veil Be Removed While Dwelling In the Spirit World?

Obviously part of the veil is removed at death. Whether unembodied spirits in the spirit world are capable of progressing to the point where the remainder of the veil of eternity is removed is a point of speculation. Possible candidates for such a blessing include "the spirits of just men made perfect" which both Joseph Smith and Paul refer to (D&C 129:1, 3, Heb. 12:23). Specifically Paul tells us that they are an advanced group because they are part of the "general assembly of the Church of the Firstborn." Equally impressive, Joseph tells us that they constitute one of the two classes of beings which occupy "heaven." These unembodied spirits appear to enjoy special opportunities, perhaps privileges which are more refined than those available to the majority of spirits in the Spirit World. It seems unlikely that a being could be allowed into "heaven" and yet still retain the effects of the veil. Possibly a "perfected" spirit is one who has already completed the work required during our second estate and would therefore derive little benefit from the continued influence of the veil.

Will the Veil Be Removed With Resurrection?

Undoubtedly, those who are resurrected to live in the celestial kingdom will enjoy their premortal memories.

Whether this restoration occurs abruptly as a consequence of the resurrection itself or whether the memories are restored gradually or at a later date is unclear. Elder Charles W. Penrose believed those who are exalted would be: "clothed in white raiment, rejoicing in the presence of the Eternal whom they will recognize again as their Father; for the past, now shut out by the veil of the flesh, will come back to them, and all their former history will return to their minds; *those memories which were shut out by tabernacling in the flesh will come back again*, and all their past experience upon the earth and in the Spirit World will be fresh to their minds, never to fade away. Then will they comprehend God, being quickened in Him and by Him, dwelling in His presence and filled with the fullness of His glory, for ever and ever" (JD 23:162; italics added). Elder Neal A. Maxwell observes that we must currently: "wait upon the restoration of our premortal memories and such other bestowals as may accompany our resurrected status" (*Even As I Am*, p. 55).

Will the Veil Be Removed At the Second Coming?

Through the scriptures, we learn about many of the events associated with the Second Coming of the Lord. Specifically, we are told that at the proper time: "the curtain of heaven [shall] be unfolded, as a scroll is unfolded after it is rolled up, and the face of the Lord shall be unveiled" (D&C 88:95; see also Revelation 6:14) so that "every eye shall see Him" (Revelation 1:7). Certainly a portion of the veil is dissolved at that moment. But we ask: "Will our premortal memories be instantly restored? Will we clearly see heavenly beings and know Satan and all his followers for what they are? Will our hearts become transparent?" The answers to these questions may depend upon the specific state of existence we are in at that point. At least four different classes of beings will be involved.

The Veil and the Unrighteous Who Are Living

The *unrighteous* people still *living* upon the earth will experience a burning of their physical bodies. "And prepare for the revelation which is to come, when the veil of the covering of my temple, in my tabernacle, which hideth the earth, shall be taken off, and all flesh shall see me together. And every corruptible thing, both of man, or of the beasts of the field, or of the fowls of the heavens, or of the fish of the sea, that dwells upon all the face of the earth, shall be consumed; And also that of element shall melt with fervent heat" (D&C 101:23-25). "For, behold, the day cometh, that shall burn as an oven; and all the proud, yea, and all that do wickedly, shall be stubble: and the day that cometh shall burn them up" (Mal. 4:1; see also D&C 29:9).

The bodies of these unrighteous persons die and their spirits are dispatched to eventually dwell in the darkened portion of the spirit world. "And the wicked shall go away into unquenchable fire, and their end no man knoweth on earth, nor ever shall know, until they come before me in judgment (D&C 43:33; see also 138:20-22, 30).

The Unrighteous Who Are Dead

Those whose bodies are burned at the Second Coming will join the spirits of the *unrighteous dead* who are already dwelling in the "unquenchable fire" spoken of. "These are they who are thrust down to hell. These are they who shall not be redeemed from the devil until the last resurrection, until the Lord, even Christ the Lamb, shall have finished his work" (D&C 76:84-85). They are "the spirits of men who are to be judged, and are found under condemnation; And these are the rest of the dead; and they live not again until the thousand years are ended, neither again, until the end of the earth" (D&C 88:101).

President Joseph Fielding Smith elaborated upon their activities during that time: "All liars, and sorcerers, and adulterers and all who love and make a lie, shall not receive the resurrection at this time, but for a thousand years shall be thrust down into hell where they shall suffer the wrath of God until they pay the price of their sinning, if it is possible, by the things which they shall suffer... This suffering will be a means of cleansing or purifying." (*Doctrines of Salvation*, 2:297-298; see also D&C 19:16-18). It seems likely that the veil will persist for these suffering spirits.

The Veil and the Righteous Who Are Dead

The righteous are blessed when the Savior comes: "And they who have slept in their graves shall come forth, for their graves shall be opened; and they also shall be caught up to meet Him in the midst of the pillar of heaven. They are Christ's, the first fruits, they who shall descend with Him first, and they who are on the earth and in their graves, who are first caught up to meet Him" (D&C 88:97-98).

It appears that the *righteous dead* are resurrected and literally rise up into the air to accompany the Lord as He descends to the earth (see D&C 84:100). As recipients of the first resurrection, it is probable that they will experience a complete disintegration of the veil within their lives.

The Veil and The Righteous Who Are Living

"The *saints that are upon the earth*, who are alive, shall be quickened and be caught up to meet [Jesus Christ]" (D&C 88:96). "[H]e that liveth in righteousness [at the Second Coming] shall be changed in the twinkling of an eye" (D&C 43:32). Some people may assume that this "quickening" or this "change" constitutes resurrection. However, we are told that individuals who "liveth when the Lord shall come" will "die" at some later time (D&C 63:50). Which also means they would be resurrected later as well.

We recall that terrestrial beings will occupy the earth for the 1000-year millennium. They will raise children and perform temple work among other things. It appears that the "quickening" or "change" is simply an elevation from a fallen-world telestial state to a more advanced terrestial state. If so, it seems likely that at least a portion of the veil would persist, primarily for the terrestrial mortals who undergo their probationary periods during the millennial reign. But the veil separating us from the Savior will be rent: "For they that are wise and have received the truth, and have taken the Holy Spirit for their guide, and have not been deceived verily I say unto you, they shall not be hewn down and cast into the fire, but shall abide the day [of the Second Coming]. And the earth shall be given unto them for an inheritance; and they shall multiply and wax strong, and their children shall grow up without sin unto salvation. *For the Lord shall be in their midst*, and His glory shall be upon them, and He will be their king and their lawgiver" (D&C 45:57-59; italics added).

AWAITING THE DAY

So we await the day when the veils are dropped, but there is much to do. We must be busily engaged, interacting with the veils every moment of every day. We strive to follow the Lord's counsel: "And verily I say unto thee that thou shalt lay aside the things of this world, and seek for the things of a better" (D&C 25:10). For we know that "this world" will soon pass away and the veil currently concealing "the things of a better," will become a memory. As a memory, the veil will simply join the multitude of other memories (currently forgotten) which will engulf us at that day. Then as "children of light" (1 Thes. 5:5) we will join the "Father of lights" (James 1:17) in eternal unveiled light and glory.

BIBLIOGRAPHY

The Church of Jesus Christ of Latter-day Saints. *The Life and Teachings of Jesus & His Apostles*, Salt Lake City, 1978.
Journal of Discourses, (abbreviated JD) 26 vols., ed. J. Watt. Liverpool, 1854-1886.
Lectures on Faith, Salt Lake City, 1903.
Juvenile Instructor, Salt Lake City, 1892.
Teachings of the Latter-day Prophets, Salt Lake City, 1986

Benson, Ezra Taft. *The Teaching of Ezra Taft Benson*, Salt Lake City, 1988.

Cannon, George Q. *Gospel Truth*. Jerreld L. Newquist, comp. Salt Lake City, 1987.

Hunter, Howard W. *The Teachings of Howard W. Hunter*, Clyde J. Williams, comp., Salt Lake City, 1997.

Jung, Carl. *Man and His Symbols*, New York, 1964.

Kimball, Spencer W. *The Teachings of Spencer W. Kimball*, Edward L. Kimball, comp., Salt Lake City, 1982.

Lee, Harold B. *The Teaching of Harold B. Lee*, Clyde J. Williams, comp., Salt Lake City, 1996.
Stand Ye in Holy Places. Salt Lake City, 1974.

Madsen, Truman. "Timeless Questions, Gospel Insights," Audio Cassette.

Maxwell Neal A. *All These Things Shall Give Thee Experience*, Salt Lake City, 1980.
A Wonderful Flood of Light, Salt Lake City, 1990.
Men and Women of Christ, Salt Lake City, 1991.

McConkie, Bruce R. *The Mortal Messiah*, 5 vols. Salt Lake City, 1980.
A New Witness for the Articles of Faith. Salt Lake City, 1985.
Doctrines of the Restoration, Sermons and Writings of Bruce R. McConkie, ed. Mark E. McConkie, Salt Lake City, 1989.

McConkie, Joseph Fielding. "Understanding Personal Revelation," Audio Cassette.

McKay, David O. *Gospel Ideals.* Salt Lake City, 1976.

Nurturing Faith Through the Book of Mormon. 24th Annual Sidney B. Sperry Symposium, Salt Lake City, 1995.

Packer, Boyd K. *"That All May Be Edified" Talks, Sermons and Commentary* by Boyd K. Packer, Salt Lake City, 1982.
The Things of the Soul, Salt Lake City, 1996.

Pratt, Parley P. *Key to the Science of Theology*, Salt Lake City, 1978.

Roberts, B.H. ed. *History of the Church*, 7 vols.,. Salt Lake City, 1978.

Smith, Joseph, *Teachings of the Prophet Joseph Smith*, comp. Joseph Fielding Smith. Salt Lake City, 1976. *The Words of Joseph Smith*, eds. Andrew F. Ehat and Lyndon W. Cook. Provo, 1980.

Smith, Joseph F. *Gospel Doctrine*. Salt Lake City, 1977.

Smith, Joseph Fielding. *Doctrines of Salvation*, 3 vols. Salt Lake City, 1954-1956.
Answers to Gospel Questions, 5 vols. Salt Lake City, 1979.
The Way to Perfection, Salt Lake City, 1968.

Stuy, Brian, ed. *Collected Discourses*, 5 vols.; Sandy, Utah, 1987-1992.

Snow, Lorenzo. *Teachings of Lorenzo Snow*, Williams, Clyde J., comp., Salt Lake City, 1984.

Taylor John. *The Gospel Kingdom*, ed. G. Homer Durham. Salt Lake City 1987.

Whitney, Orson F., *Life of Heber C. Kimball*. Salt Lake City, 1888; 2nd ed., 1945.

Woodruff, Wilford. *The Discourses of Wilford Woodruff*, ed. G. Homer Durham. Salt Lake City, 1968.

Young, Brigham. *Discourses of Brigham Young*, comp. J. Widtsoe. Salt Lake City, 1954.

Index

"heart reflexes", 108-109
influence of, 104-112
is very complex, 126
righteous, 100
veil of, 99-112
veil—removal of, 169
Holland, Jeffrey, R., 72
Hunter, Howard, W., 36, 72

– J –
Jesus Christ, awaits at the veil, 72
is the perfect example, 147
is truth, 146
temptation, 80-83
John the Revelator, 62, 63
Jung, Carl, 102

– K –
Kimball, Heber C., account of Spirit World visit, 24
Kimball, Spencer, W., 52, 60, 72

– L –

Lee, Harold, B. 10, 11, 152
Listening, to others reveals the contents of our hearts, 151

– M –
Marriage, creates conflicts, 118
Materialism, 83, 86-90
needs and wants, 88
Maxwell, Neal A., 4, 47, 168, 175
McConkie, Bruce R., 43